Christianity and Secularism

Consider Christianity Series, Volume 2

by

Elgin L. Hushbeck, Jr.

Third Edition

Energion Publications
Cantonment, FL
2025

This edition is a corrected and expanded version.

Cover Design by Jason Neufeld, http://www.jasonneufelddesign.com.
Cover photograph courtesy of the National Space Science Data Center.

ISBN: 978-1-63199-933-8
eISBN: 978-1-63199-934-5

Energion Publications
1241 Conference Rd
Cantonment, FL 32533
.https://www.energion.com
pubs@energion.com

To

Hannelore P. L. Hushbeck

My Wife, Partner, Companion
and the
Love of my Life

TABLE OF CONTENTS

Acknowledgments

As has been said, no book, especially one such as this, is a single person's work. This book results from many years of research and countless discussions. First and foremost, I want to thank my wife and family for putting up with me as I researched and wrote this book.

I can say without hesitation that had it not been for their love, support, understanding, and encouragement, I could not have written this book.

I also want to thank Inge Johnson for the time she has spent reading and correcting several early drafts of this work and for the comments she has given me. My special thanks go to my readers, Starlett Ichsan Johnson, Tim Munson, David C. Rimoldi, and Steven B. Sherman. They gave me invaluable help on the final versions of this manuscript.

Others who deserve to be singled out for their comments and inputs, both formal and informal, are Courtney Duncan, Brooks Thomas, Jeff Srinivasan, Tom Meehan, Rob Kursinski, Don Spitizmesser, and Joe Grahle. Much of what is good in this book results from their input and criticisms. Any mistakes or errors, however, are mine.

In addition, I want to give a special thanks to one of my professors at Simon Greenleaf University, Dallas Willard, who, at a crucial time, encouraged me to continue and to publish. I also want to thank Roger Schmidt, one of my early professors in religious studies, and Sidney Allen for helping me see things logically.

I would also like to thank the many people who so kindly (and even who sometimes not so kindly) gave me feedback and comments on the earlier editions of this book. Finally, I would like to thank many people, particularly Larry and Diane Nixon, my editor, Henry Neufeld, and my wife, friend, and companion, Hanna, for pushing me to finish this new edition.

Preface to 2nd edition

While God does not change, the defense of Christianity does. Critics are constantly coming up with new arguments. Actually, they usually dust off old arguments long after they have been refuted and discarded, but the net effect is the same. What was not an issue yesterday suddenly becomes the latest reason why Christianity is false.

On the other side of the spectrum is the discovery of new evidence. Researchers find new manuscripts and archaeological discoveries continue to broaden our understanding of the ancient world and support the Biblical account. I have revised this second edition considering some of these developments.

Since the first edition of *Consider Christianity*, several new books have been published attacking the Christian faith. Most have constructed straw men, which they then proceed to knock down. Because of this, they are hard to take seriously.

One notable exception to this is Michael Martin's *The Case Against Christianity*. While Martin still fails to make his case, he has at least taken some of the defenders of Christianity seriously.

As such, I have added comments on Martin's arguments at appropriate places in this edition, along with some of the other recent books.

Elgin L Hushbeck
Redlands, California June 2005

Preface to 3rd edition

I began writing what ultimately became this book in the mid-1980s. A lot has changed since then. In early 2000, I revised and updated this book, adding enough new material to split it into two books, this one and *Evidence for the Bible*.

Now, 15 years later, with plans for an audio edition and the book being translated into other languages, my publisher and I believe it is time for a new edition.

This update was not as significant as the second edition. There is no splitting one book into two this time. Most changes involve improving my writing, as my skills have improved over the years. I added some comments here and tweaked an argument there. In a few places, I addressed nuances missed in the first two editions or which have become more relevant over the years.

The recent developments since the earlier editions have further strengthened the belief that Christianity is a rational, reasonable, and relevant religion.

Elgin Hushbeck
Wausau, WI
Nov 2024

How To
Read This Book

The Consider Christianity Series aims to present a systematic defense of the Christian Faith. Volume One focused on the evidence for the Bible. This book looks at some broader issues. Because of this step-by-step approach, different people will want to read this book differently.

This book is written with non-Christians in mind and tries to address a vast range of questions and objections. Since not everyone will start this book with the same beliefs, not everyone will want to begin with Chapter 1 or even read the chapters in order.

For example, Chapter 2 deals with the supernatural. If this is not an issue, you may skip this chapter. In short, while this book is a step-by-step argument for the Christian faith, you might only want to read the areas where you have questions.

Below is a brief description of each chapter of the book, giving you an idea of the questions addressed so you can easily find the issues that interest you.

PART I - Christianity

Some people think that religion is something that other people believe. Yet, what is religion? This chapter demonstrates that religion is universal; thus, everybody has a religion. The question is not, as often stated, 'Am I going to have a religion?' but rather, 'Which religion is true?'

The rejection of the supernatural forms the basis for much criticism of Christianity. This chapter looks at the existence of the supernatural and critiques secularism's rejection of it. The chapter shows that critics do not base their objections on evidence but on assumptions. The chapter then gives evidence for the supernatural.

Despite our strong Christian heritage, many people do not know what Christianity actually teaches. Some views of Christianity are radically different from what Christians have historically believed. This chapter briefly surveys the basic teachings of Christianity on God, Jesus, Salvation, and the Bible. The chapter dispels the myth that the Bible is so vague that everything is just a matter of interpretation.

Many people say they love God but don't like how the Church has messed things up. This chapter looks at the true nature of the Church, along with the Church's role in history. While the Church is not perfect, it is by no means the evil institution that some claim.

PART II - Jesus Christ

Central to Christianity is the life of Jesus Christ. Who was He? The critics have many theories, and this chapter examines them individually. Using primarily the writings of the early critics of Christianity, the chapter shows that the theories of modern critics do not stand up to scrutiny. In fact, from the early critics, we see a picture of Jesus coming close to the Jesus of the Gospels. In short, we see that the only reasonable answer to the identity of Jesus is Peter's: "You are the Christ."

The Bible's most essential teaching is Jesus's death and resurrection, which is also the most questioned. Critics have long sought an alternative explanation and have put forth many. After examining the Gospels and finding that they present a consistent account of Jesus' death and resurrection, we look at the explanations put forth by the critics and see that they come up short. The only valid explanation is that Jesus conquered death. He is risen!

PART III - Christianity and the Modern World

So what if the Bible is true and Jesus is Lord? The Bible is over 2,000 years old. What could it say to a world of space exploration and computers? In the final chapter, we see that there is no foundation for morality apart from God. Since morality forms the basis for order in society, we need God. However, society cannot have a relationship with God; the relationship must be personal. Each one of us must decide for ourselves whether or not to accept Christ as our savior.

Introduction: The Secularization of Society

'Come now, let us reason together,' says the Lord.

(Isaiah 1:18)

When people stop believing in God, they don't believe in nothing – they believe in anything.[1]

(GK Chesterton)

Western civilization is rapidly casting off the chains of religious oppression and moving towards a society based on reason and science instead of faith and superstition. This view is, at least, the image we are presented with by popular culture.[2] While polls show that most people still believe in God, the number of people who say religion is very important in their lives declined by nearly a third between 1952 and 1978.[3] By the mid-nineties, weekly church attendance had dropped to only 37%.[4]

1   While commonly cite as directly from Chesterton, the actual quote is most likely a combination of two of Chesterton's quotes from his Father Brown stories. See www.chesterton.org/ceases-to-worship/
2   The term popular culture is used here as a rather broad term which covers the common and underlying presuppositions and beliefs which are represented in the normal channels of mass communications such as network television, movies, music, etc. As with any broad term there are of course exceptions to the general rule. This is especially true when one is dealing with a country as large and diverse as the United States.
3   George Gallup Jr and David Poling, *The Search for America's Faith* (Nashville: Abrindon, 1980) p. appendix K.
4   George Barna, *The State of the Church, 2005* (Ventura, Ca, The Barna Group, 2005)

Probably more important is the growing attitude among some that religion is a unique phenomenon and, as such, should play no role in one's public life.

Like many things in our society, movies and TV reflect religion's changing role. Until the sixties, you could see religion playing a noticeable role in the lives of many characters, although it was a background role. Biblical stories, like *The Ten Commandments,* were the subject of major Hollywood productions.

Even when religion was not the main subject of a film, having the main character attend a church or having their pastor or priest visit was not unusual. They would express in some way their belief as important. People saw religion as a natural and integral part of life.

Today, the situation has almost completely reversed. Except in films made by religious organizations, movies rarely portray religion as a positive influence. Religious epics are practically non-existent.

Mel Gibson's *The Passion of the Christ* is a recent exception. But even here, it is notable that Gibson had trouble getting a distributor. He also had to finance the film himself and faced intense criticism for even making it.

Unlike in the past when religion was commonplace, today, most main characters no longer had any religious aspects in their lives. In fact, with most characters, it would seem awkward or unnatural to include any serious religious elements in the story.

By the 1980s, religion no longer fits with our "modern" concepts of society. When a religious character did appear, they were, with few exceptions, appear as one of two types: the radical Bible-quoting fundamentalist or the good-hearted simpleton.

The fundamentalist usually is an evangelist from the South or, perhaps, a televangelist. They frequently play the role of the villain or someone who wants to run everyone's life, often so that they can fill their pockets with money.

An example of this type of fundamentalist character is Reverend Willie Williams in the movie *Oh God.* In this movie, out of a gathering of clergy from many faiths and denominations, it was only Reverend Williams, the fundamentalist, with whom God was upset. God, in the guise of George Burns, went so far as to call him Reverend Big Mouth and a phony.

This view of the fundamentalist has, in many ways, become a stereotype. Many people see all fundamentalists in this light. Of course, some fit the stereotype, as in any large group; one can always find a few stereotypical people. But like all stereotypes, this one does not represent the vast majority but is a misleading depiction of them.

The fact that in the 1980s, the Assemblies of God denomination refused to yield to pressure from Jimmy Swaggart and expelled him demonstrates that not all fundamentalists/evangelicals place money as the prime concern.

Despite the millions of dollars Swaggart sent to the Assemblies of God each year, he received no special treatment. They expected him to follow the rules the same as everyone else. They expelled him when he refused to comply with a ruling that he does not preach after becoming involved in a sex scandal. This move cost the Assemblies of God millions in revenue.

The good-hearted simpleton, on the other hand, is someone who, although they may have good intentions, is portrayed as really being out of place in modern society. They are consistently depicted as frail and ineffectual, often having trouble coping with contemporary culture. As such, they frequently need someone to come to their rescue.

An example of the simpleton would be Father Mulcahy of the television show *MASH*. Although a very positive character, he was always somewhat helpless and out of place.

While many films have used characters like the fundamentalist or the simpleton, thus giving a negative impression of religion, a few movies have presented religion as essential and positive. Two examples would be *Chariots of Fire* and *The Mission*. Both films, however, were historical, reinforcing the notion that religion is a thing of the past.

Society's Reaction

The stereotypes found are a somewhat passive assault on religion; in other areas, the assault is much more direct. An ever-increasing number of groups, such as the American Civil Liberties Union (ACLU), closely monitor the role that religion is allowed to play in public life. They seek to ensure it does not stray beyond what they consider 'proper' limits.

As long as religion is in the context of personal faith or the past, it is acceptable or tolerated. Any suggestion, however, that religion might still play an important and relevant role in public discussion meets with reactions that range from simple disbelief to outright hostility.

The last openly religious President was George Bush. His openness about his faith and comments about God engendered reactions that showed some of this hostility. Compared with statements of earlier presidents, even as recent as Reagan and Carter, Bush's remarks were not all that unusual.

They were toned down when compared to some past presidents. But in the current climate of growing hostility to religion, Bush's statements were often criticized as 'dangerous,' 'alarming,' and 'deeply troubling.'

It is not simply a matter of society turning its back on religion, for a segment of society in general, and government in particular, are becoming increasingly hostile. There is a conscious effort made by many groups to oppose religion wherever and whenever they can.

Christmas and Easter, for example, have become the seasons of lawsuits over nativity scenes and crosses. Long ago, Christmas and Easter vacations were renamed Winter and Spring breaks in most schools. The traditional Christmas nativity plays now have non-religious themes.

Christmas has become an almost entirely secular holiday, with all references to Christianity removed. It has become merely a day of celebration, a day of celebration without anything to celebrate.

Much of American society replaced Christ with Santa Claus; TV programming is a clear example. Over the past few decades, programs that told the story of the first Christmas, the birth of Christ, have disappeared, replaced by stories concerning Santa Claus.

In fact, in many ways, Santa Claus has replaced God himself. In one holiday movie, *One Magic Christmas*, an angel takes a little girl to the only person who might be able to answer her prayers. The angel does not take her to God but to Santa Claus.

While she is visiting Santa, we discover that when good people die, they do not go to heaven; they go to the North Pole to become one of Santa's helpers. Ultimately, one is unsure if the angel works for God or Santa Claus.

Problems In Schools

You can see examples of this conflict simply by watching the news during the Christmas season. One typical example occurred at the Shawnee Mission School District in Missouri. There, the superintendent of schools informed the teachers that they should celebrate Christmas as an "American Tradition."

This attitude is appropriate for a public school. However, according to one teacher, the superintendent "strongly emphasized that we should use 'winter holiday' instead of using the words Christmas or anything to do with Christ."[5]

This is not to say that the public schools have deliberately tried to undermine and destroy children's faith or that there is some dark, sinister conspiracy. Most of these 'attacks' have been subtle and indirect. They are often the unintended result of a strict adherence to the recently developed view that the First Amendment demands a separation of church and state.

5   Robert Griggs, This was part of testimony given before the Department of Education on proposed regulations for the Hatch amendment. The testimony appears in: Phyllis Schlafly, *Child Abuse in the Classroom* (Westchester, Ill, Crossway Books, 1985) p. 214

Yet a subtle, even unintentional, attack can be the most devastating. This is especially true with children who have not yet gained the critical thinking skills to evaluate them.

The British author G. K. Chesterton believed that what you say to a child is not as important as what you assume, and a child may ignore or even laugh at what you say. Still, the unstated and underlying assumptions sink in to affect the child without them even realizing it.

If a teacher were to stand before a class and teach that Christianity, as a religion, was no longer relevant to life in the 21st century, this would be a direct attack. While this has been part of some school programs,[6] this direct attack is neither the norm nor the main problem.

Instead, it is the teachings that have as their foundation the underlying assumption that religion no longer has a vital role to play in our lives. This assumption is central to public schools today.

A child goes to school to learn the skills that will allow them to function as productive members of society. Ignore something, and it must not be necessary. Children now go through at least twelve years of school, carefully being shielded from contact with religion.

So carefully are the children shielded that, in many cases, teachers give secular reasons for religious celebrations, even when this results in a distortion of history. These distortions teach that religion is no longer needed much more effectively than any direct statements could.

As some have, one might argue that we should teach about the separation of church and state so that children can understand why religion is absent. Yet, when the separation of church and state has been a source of confusion and dispute in the land's highest courts, can we really expect children to understand it?

Besides, we would still leave the impression that if religion were significant, something would be taught. Instead, we leave children with a nearly complete void concerning the world's great religions.

---

6   For one such example see, Schlafly, *Child Abuse*, p. 216

Today, few children have learned anything about the rich and varied history of even their own faith. The religions of others are, for the most part, a great mystery.

This mystery is most likely to remain as such. The lack of interest on the part of the public schools will very likely become a lack of interest in the child. Where knowledge is limited, the vacuum will be filled with stereotypes, which are usually wrong and derogatory. Thus, for many people, a Muslim is a terrorist with a bomb or a rich sultan with fifty wives. They don't know who Muhammad was or what he taught.

The teachings stemming from a strict secular attitude have troubled many parents, particularly the underlying assumptions. There are many examples of these subtle attacks.

A writing assignment in one composition textbook asked the students to write about religion. This assignment probably would not have caused problems for most people except for the specific topic. Students were asked to write, "I don't have much use for any kind of …"[7] Thus, under the guise of an English class, students were asked to formulate anti-religious attitudes.

Another example comes from a value clarification course. Teachers displayed a large poster to an elementary school class with objects of varying sizes scattered randomly. Teachers then told the children that the size of an object corresponded to that object's importance. The large items on the chart were things like Love and Home, and the smallest objects were related to religion.[8]

Value Clarification or Moral Education seems to be particularly problematic. While these names make the classes sound like essential

---

7   Kay Fradeneck, This was part of testimony given before the Department of Education on proposed regulations for the Hatch amendment. The testimony appears in: Phyllis Schlafly, *Child Abuse in the Classroom* (Westchester, Ill, Crossway Books, 1985) p. 161
8   Robert Griggs, This was part of testimony given before the Department of Education on proposed regulations for the Hatch amendment. The testimony appears in: Phyllis Schlafly, *Child Abuse in the Classroom* (Westchester, Ill, Crossway Books, 1985) p. 214

subjects for children, which they are, morals and values education often aim to change society rather than strengthen it.

Some of the people pushing Value Clarification courses realize they are attempting to reshape society and thus expect that they are likely to face strong opposition. The editors of *The Humanist* magazine wrote that,

> For some time now Moral-education programs have been conducted in the public schools, but not without vigorous opposition. Many religionists who reject moral education programs in schools maintain that secular humanism is being introduced and that this constitutes a violation of the separation of church and state. Earlier objections to sex education and the teaching of evolution drew similar criticism. In spite of strong opposition, moral education and Value Clarification programs are making rapid progress in school curricula.[9]

Some advocating the changes that have concerned many parents fully realize what they are attempting. They seek to use public schools to destroy beliefs in what they see as useless or harmful religions. John Dunphy stated this quite clearly when, at the end of an article in *The Humanist* attacking Christianity, he wrote:

> I am convinced that the battle for humankind's future must be waged and won in the public schools classroom by teachers who correctly perceive their role as the proselytizers of a new faith: a religion of humanity that recognizes and respects the spark of what theologians call divinity in every human being. These teachers must embody the same selfless dedication as the most rabid fundamentalist preachers, for they will be ministers of another sort, utilizing a classroom instead of the pulpit to convey humanist values in whatever subject they teach, regardless of the education level – preschool day care or large state university. The classroom must and will become an arena of conflict between the old and new – the rotting corpse of Christianity, together with all the adjacent evils and misery,

---

9   *Moral Education and Secular Humanism: A Symposium,* The Humanist, Nov/Dec 1978

and the new faith of Humanism, resplendent in its promise of a world in which the never-realized Christian ideal of 'love thy neighbor' will finally be achieved… It will undoubtedly be a long, arduous, painful, struggle replete with much sorrow and tears, but humanism will emerge triumphant.[10]

Again, I must emphasize that this is not evidence of some dark conspiracy. These people do what they think is best for our children and society. Still, it does demonstrate that, at least for some, this is a conscious effort.

There are two problems with this effort. The first problem is the tactics employed to achieve this goal, particularly how parents are often seen as problematic and kept out of the process. The second is that many of the issues dealt with in these classes are inherently religious, as we will see later. They are not, in reality, stamping out religion, just replacing one religious view with another.

An example of the first problem was the National Educational Association's (NEA) response to the Hatch Amendment in the 1980s. The Hatch Amendment grew out of parental complaints about what was happening in many classrooms. Simply stated, the Hatch Amendment required that a school obtain parental permission before they give a child a psychological or psychiatric examination or before probing into a child's personal or family life.

After seven years of delay, the Department of Education finally issued the regulations to enforce the Hatch Amendment, and the NEA strongly opposed them, stating,

> Enforced as currently written, the Reagan Administration's "Child privacy" regulations would mandate that all instructional material – including teachers' manual, films, and tapes – must be made available for parental inspection.[11]

---

10 John J. Dunphy, *A Religion for a New Age The Humanist,* Nov/Dec 1983, p. 26
11 *NEA Newsletter,* Apr 16, 1984

Many parents might wonder why teaching materials used for their children's instruction should not be available for inspection. What is it that the parents should not be allowed to see?

The second problem is that many of the issues are inherently religious. Beginning in the late 1940s, the Supreme Court reinterpreted the First Amendment to ban Bible reading from the classroom. Organized prayer was banned in the classroom and at graduation and sporting events.

One cannot post a copy of the Ten Commandments in public school classrooms, even though they are essential to understanding the history of Western Civilizations. The effect of all these rulings is to remove Christian views from the school. What remains is a one-sided debate in which the cards have been stacked in favor of secularism and against the traditional views grounded in religions.

This systematic exclusion of religion in general, and Christianity in particular, was demonstrated in a study of children's textbooks by New York University professor of psychology Paul Vitz. In his research for the National Institute of Education, Vitz studied approximately 70-75 percent of the social studies textbooks for grades one through six and all the Basal readers for California and Texas. While only two states, these are used by many other states as guides in purchasing their textbooks.

Social studies texts aim to introduce children to the world in which they live. Starting close to home, they move out to the local community, states, nation, and finally, the world in both the contemporary and historical sense. Yet in his study, Vitz found that not only is the role of religion in modern society discounted, but,

> That not one of the forty books totaling ten thousand pages had one text reference to a primary religious activity occurring in representative contemporary American life.[12]

---

12 Paul C Vitz, *Censorship: Evidence of Bias in our Children's Textbooks* (Ann Arbor, MI, Servant Books, 1986) p. 11

From the point of view of children learning from these books, religion had ceased to exist in America. In many cases, textbook writers changed history to remove any connection to religion. Vitz cites some straightforward examples,

> Other examples of the washing-out of religion are such explanations as "Pilgrims are people who make long trips" or "Mardi Gras is the end of winter celebration. "…it is common in these books to treat Thanksgiving without explaining to whom the Pilgrims gave thanks… One mother wrote me that her first grade son was told by his teacher that at Thanksgiving the Pilgrims gave thanks to the Indians! When she complained to the principal that Thanksgiving was a feast to thank God, the principal replied that her position "was just opinion and not documented fact" and therefore they could not teach it. The principal said that "they could only teach what was contained in the history books."[13]

As for the Basal readers, Vitz found that a very similar situation existed,

> When one looks at the total sample of 670 pieces in the Basal readers, the following findings stand out. Serious Judeo-Christian religious motivation is featured nowhere. References to Christianity or Judaism are rare and generally superficial. Protestantism is almost entirely excluded, at least for whites. In contrast primitive and pagan religions as well as magic, get considerable emphasis. Patriotism is close to non-existent in the sample. Likewise any appreciation of business success is grossly unrepresented. Traditional roles for both men and women receives virtually no support.[14]

Overall, Vitz concludes that these textbooks, which public schools use to introduce children to the world around them,

13   Paul C Vitz, *Censorship: Evidence of Bias in our Children's Textbooks* (Ann Arbor, MI, Servant Books, 1986) pp. 18-19. From time to time, I have tested this by asking my college level students what they were taught about the first Thanksgiving. While not a rigorous survey, a significant percentage has said that they were taught that the pilgrims were giving thanks to the Indians.

14   Paul C Vitz, *Censorship: Evidence of Bias in our Children's Textbooks* (Ann Arbor, MI, Servant Books, 1986) pp. 75-6

Commonly exclude the history, heritage, belief, and values of millions of Americans ... those who are committed to their religious traditions – at the very least as an important part of the historical record – are not represented .[15]

In 1987, some parents objected to bias in their children's textbooks. Initially, they sought and received permission from the principal to use an alternate set of state-approved textbooks. The local school board prohibited using alternate textbooks and expelled their children from school. The parents filed suit to allow their children to use the alternate textbooks.

The original judge in the case ruled in favor of the parents. He ruled the problem was the overall bias and not the content of any particular story. The problem passages "would be rendered inoffensive or less offensive, in a more balanced context."[16]

Even though the parents complained about the restriction of ideas and wished only for a more balanced treatment, the mass media fell back on the stereotypes discussed earlier. They labeled these parents as book-burning fundamentalists trying to censor the public school curriculum. In the end, an appellate court overturned the case.

This ruling left the parents with only two options. They could accept a distorted curriculum undermining their values and beliefs or remove their children from the public schools their taxes support. These parents chose to remove their children from public schools.

They are not the only ones. Due to such problems, many parents opted not to fight the public schools; instead, they placed their children in private schools or even home-schooling. From 1970 to 1985, the school-age population declined in the U.S., with public school enrollment dropping 17 percent. Yet hundreds of thousands of parents placed their children into private schools in this same period, causing their enrollment to rise by six percent.

---

15   Paul C Vitz, *Censorship: Evidence of Bias in our Children's Textbooks* (Ann Arbor, MI, Servant Books, 1986) p 77

16   *Phi Delta Kappan*, 68:453, Feb 1987, pg 452

The Conflict Continues

Some significant changes occurred between the 1993 publication of the first edition of this book and the second edition in 2006. The most obvious has been that the conflict grew, or at least became more noticeable, including more than just 'fundamentalist religious views.' It now included much of the Judeo-Christian tradition, which has helped define Western civilization.

Those objecting to secularism in the 1980s were written off by many as simply "fundamentalist." When a court ruled the Pledge of Allegiance unconstitutional, many thought the demands for complete secularization went too far.

Because of this, it was common to see discussions of the "culture war," which refers to the ongoing battle over the nature of the American culture. Will the culture that America has had since its founding be allowed to continue? Will a small minority[17] using the courts and relatively new interpretations of the Constitution be able to force society to follow secular values and beliefs? The outcome here is still uncertain.

Another significant factor has been a two-fold change in Christianity. One part is the decline discussed above, which appears to have bottomed out and even reversed to some extent. Weekly church attendance has grown from a low of 37 percent in 1996 to 45 percent in 2005.[18]

Likewise, those who regularly read the Bible have grown from a low of 31 percent in 1995 to 45 percent in 2005.[19] In addition to this change in the overall numbers, Christianity has shifted away

17 According to polls in 2005, atheist and agnostics make up only 10 percent of the population. Evangelical and Born Again Christians make up 40 percent, with another 39% Christians who do not fall into these two categories. The remaining 12 percent make up the other faiths, such as Jews, Buddhist, Mormons, Jehovah's Witnesses, Muslims, etc. [18]

18 George Barna, *The State of the Church, 2005* (Ventura, Ca, The Barna Group, 2005) p 7

19 George Barna, *The State of the Church, 2005* (Ventura, Ca, The Barna Group, 2005), p 11

from the more religiously liberal mainline denominations towards conservative non-denominational churches. As a result, in 2005, born-again Christians now constitute a majority of Christians attending church each week.[20]

By the time of the third edition, the results were more mixed. Overall, Church attendance dropped again, and in 2021, it was 22 percent. However, Millennials and Gen X showed increased attendance, with Millennials showing the most significant increase, reaching 39% in 2022.[21]

The situation in the media also seems more mixed. The negative portrayals have diminished, and some positive portrayals do appear. For example, in the show *Seal Team*, the number two man in the team is a man of faith, and his struggles are taken seriously. Perhaps most surprising are the *Fast and Furious* movies in which the main character is defined by family, and the movies normally end with a family dinner that starts with grace.

Still, the overall portrayal is not positive. Studies show that those most affected by the secularization of public schools and mass media are, not surprisingly, the most likely to reject Christianity.[22]

Despite these positive developments, since the publication of the second edition, the situation has worsened. With the rise of a Woke culture that is anti-Christian, those with traditional Christian views faced growing harassment and sometimes even legal actions.

In 2017, the Supreme Court in Masterpiece Cakeshop, Ltd, v Colorado Civil Rights Commission, faced the question of whether a Christian baker, Jack Phillips, could be forced to use his skills to create a cake that violated his religious beliefs. The court found that,

> some of the commissioners at the Commission's formal, public hearings endorsed the view that religious beliefs cannot

20   George Barna, *The State of the Church, 2005* (Ventura, Ca, The Barna Group, 2005), p 7

21   Barna Group, *A New Chapter in Millennial Church Attendance* August 4, 2022, https://www.barna.com/research/church-attendance-2022/

22   George Barna, *The State of the Church, 2005* (Ventura, Ca, The Barna Group, 2005), p 29

legitimately be carried into the public sphere or commercial domain, disparaged Phillips' faith as despicable and characterized it as merely rhetorical, and compared his invocation of his sincerely held religious beliefs to defenses of slavery and the Holocaust. No commissioners objected to the comments.[23]

As a result of this and other mistreatments, the court ruled 7-2 that,

> the Commission's treatment of Phillips' case violated the State's duty under the First Amendment not to base laws or regulations on hostility to a religion or religious viewpoint. The government, consistent with the Constitution's guarantee of free exercise, cannot impose regulations that are hostile to the religious beliefs of affected citizens and cannot act in a manner that passes judgment upon or presupposes the illegitimacy of religious beliefs and practices.[24]

The Supreme Court ruling should have settled the issue. Christians could not be subject to anti-Christian hostility by the government. Yet, it did not end the matter; others faced more carefully crafted harassment.

It did not even end for Jack Phillips. On the day the Supreme Court announced they would hear his case, another customer requested a cake that violated Phillips's religious beliefs. Again, the commission found him guilty, and as I write the third edition, his case is currently on appeal.

Nor is it just lawsuits. Overt discrimination is increasing. George Yancey, professor of sociology at Baylor University, found that Americans, in general, dislike conservative Christians even more than Muslims, leading him to ask,

> So it's fair to say that if we're concerned about anti-Muslim prejudice, then we should also be concerned about an-

---

23   Masterpiece Cakeshop, Ltd., et al. v. Colorado Civil Rights Commission et al. https://www.supremecourt.gov/opinions/17pdf/16-111_j4el.pdf

24   Masterpiece Cakeshop, Ltd., et al. v. Colorado Civil Rights Commission et al. https://www.supremecourt.gov/opinions/17pdf/16-111_j4el.pdf

ti-Christian prejudice—at least prejudice against conservative Christians.[25]

In a survey of academics, he found that,

> half would be less willing to hire a fundamentalist, and almost two in five would be less willing to hire an evangelical. The academics answering my survey explicitly stated they would discriminate against a job candidate who is a conservative Protestant.[26]

Acts of violence against Christians and churches are growing as well. In one report, from May 2020 to November 2022, there were 230 attacks on Catholic Churches in 39 states.[27]

While a growing problem here, violence against Christians in the United States is well below the levels of persecution they face worldwide, which is also growing. According to one study, in 2019, the persecution of Christians for their faith resulted in 2,983 deaths and 488 Churches and other Christian buildings attacked.[28]

Often, this persecution is not because of any serious consideration of the evidence for or against Christianity. Instead, like most prejudice, it is simply a blind acceptance of the stereotypes and distorted views these sources present.

---

25   George Yancey, *Is there really Anti-Chrisian Discrimination in America?* The Gospel Coalition, August 19, 2019 https://www.thegospelcoalition.org/article/anti-christian-discrimination-america/
26   George Yancey, *Is there really Anti-Chrisian Discrimination in America?* The Gospel Coalition, August 19, 2019 https://www.thegospelcoalition.org/article/anti-christian-discrimination-america/
27   Tommy Valentine, Tracker: Over 200 Attacks on U.S. Catholic Churches Since May 2020
Catholic Vote.org Updates November 10, 2022, https://catholicvote.org/tracker-church-attacks/
28   Violence against Christians surges globally, data shows more than 9k attacks on churches in 2019, RNS Press Release Distribution Service, January 15, 2020, https://religionnews.com/2020/01/15/violence-against-christians-surges-globally-data-shows-more-than-9k-attacks-on-churches-in-2019/

An alternative trend is seen in Bible sales, which have significantly increased from 9.7 million in 2019 to over 14 million in 2023. The first 10 months of 2024 showed Bible sales were on track for an additional 22% increase over 2023 sales.

Likewise, Faith-based entertainment has grown in popularity and even become mainstream. Whether this is a momentary blip or will become a long-term trend remains unclear as I write this.

The first volume in this series addressed some of these distortions regarding the Bible. This book will address many common misconceptions and errors surrounding religion in general and Christianity in particular. It will also examine the evidence for who Jesus was and the resurrection. Finally, it will examine the question of whether Christianity is relevant in the modern world.

As with the first book, answering every question and objection in these areas would be impossible. I hope what will be clear is that contrary to the claim of many secularists, Christianity is not an outdated and possibly even harmful religion but rather a rational, reasonable, and relevant faith in the 21st century.

Part I

Christianity

1

A Rose By Any Other Name

I should say that Christianity has hitherto been the most portentous of presumptions.

(Friedrich Nietzsche)[29]

The time has come for widespread recognition of the radical changes in religious beliefs throughout the modern world. The time is past for mere revision of traditional attitudes. Science and economic changes have disrupted the old beliefs ... doctrines and methods which have lost their significance and which are powerless to solve the problem of human living in the Twentieth Century.

(Humanist Manifesto I)[30]

O N A HOT, sweltering, mid-July day in 1925, two legal giants met to wage an epic battle in the small Tennessee town of Dayton. The subject of the trial seemed trivial to some. Had a young biology teacher violated a state ban by teaching evolution? The Scopes trial was to have been a simple test case set up by the fledgling American Civil Liberties Union (ACLU). Ultimately, it became the climactic battle in a war that had been seething for years.

Both sides quickly realized the stakes were too high to entrust to unknown small-town lawyers. The big guns were brought in.

---

29 Friedrich Nietzsche, *Beyond Good and Evil* (New York, MacMillan Company, 1907) p. 84

30 *Humanist Manifesto I* in *Humanist Manifesto I and II* ed. Paul Kurtz (Buffalo, NY: Prometheus Books, 1973) p. 7

William Jennings Bryan, a three-time Democratic presidential candidate, advocate for the working class, and well-known orator and defender of the Bible, was the lawyer for the prosecution. For the defense, the ACLU hired one of the most famous defense lawyers in American history, Clarence Darrow.

These two legal giants met, and the nation stood by transfixed. Bryan argued that evolution was false and should not be taught. Darrow argued that freedom and liberty required that students hear both views so that they could decide for themselves.

Bryan won in the courtroom, and the court found Scopes guilty, fining him $100. Yet, in the court of public opinion, Bryan lost and lost big. Perhaps it was symbolic of the defeat that Bryan died a week after the trial. The battle was over.

Before the trial, the question of creation and evolution had been the subject of a lot of discussion and debate. Looking through the religious section of the *Los Angeles Times* on any given Saturday during the early Twenties, you would have almost certainly found advertisements for several sermons and lectures on the subject.

This debate had been raging off and on for the sixty years since Darwin proposed his theory. After the trial, these advertisements virtually disappeared. By the Thirties, the religious section had dwindled to only a few pages.

In the decades since the trial, society has gradually reshaped itself to fit a secular blueprint. Many now see religion as a harmful and dangerous influence. The Oxford Companion to the Supreme Court describes this shift as "rather than an indispensable foundation of civilized society … religion had come to be seen as a reactionary obstacle to secular progress."[31]

While the role of traditional religion in public life has continued to lessen, distressing many critics, and despite many predictions concerning its imminent demise,[32] religion has not faded

---

31   *The Oxford Companion to the Supreme Court of the United States,* s.v. *Religion* ed. Kermit L. Hall

32   For an example see John J Dunphy, *A Religion for a New Age The*

into oblivion. In fact, quite the opposite; recently, there has been renewed interest and growth in religion.[33]

Most people in America profess a religious belief of one sort or another; they also accept the secularization of society. Not only do they believe this is proper, but it is also required since the Constitution calls for the separation of church and state. Yet, the Constitution does not mention a "separation of church and state." Instead, the First Amendment states,

> Congress shall make no law respecting an establishment of religion, or prohibiting the free exercise thereof; or abridging the freedom of speech, or of the press; or the right of the people peaceably to assemble, and to petition the government for a redress of grievances.

Where do we get the phrase "separation of church and state" if it is not in the Constitution?

Many feared losing the recently acquired religious freedoms in the latter part of the eighteenth century. This concern was heightened by publications such as *An Appeal to the Public in Behalf of the Church of England in America,* written by Thomas Chandler in 1767.

While Chandler mainly called for a resident bishop, some saw this as the first step in making the Church of England the official church in America. Others saw the Catholic Church and the power of the Pope as a threat.

Fear of a national church that would restrict or even eliminate other churches strengthened the Disestablishment Movement. When the new Congress was drafting the Bill of Rights in 1789, some suggested that the religious section of the First Amendment read, "*no religion shall be established by law*" or "*no national religion shall be established.*" Ultimately, these suggestions were broadened as Congress adopted the wording to read, "*Congress shall make no*

Humanist, Jan/Feb 1983 p. 26

33 George Barna, *The Barna Report 1992-93* (Ventura CA: Regal Books, 1992) p. 24

law respecting an establishment of religion, or prohibiting the free exercise thereof." The states ratified this amendment, and it became law in 1791.[34]

Some have claimed that even though the First Amendment does not have the words "separation of church and state," this is the meaning that the founding fathers intended. However, there are significant problems with such a view.

The historian Paul Johnson wrote that this modern understanding of the First Amendment "would have astonished and angered the founding fathers."[35] He went on to point out that Madison "saw an important role for religious feeling in shaping a republican society"[36] and that

> the same can be said for the great majority of those who signed the Declaration of Independence, who attended the Constitutional Convention, and who framed the First Amendment.[37]

Another problem with this view is that Congress, the day after approving the amendment, which some now claim was to separate religion from government, passed a resolution calling for a national day of prayer and thanksgiving. Is it reasonable to think that the people who wanted a complete separation the next day would pass a resolution saying, "We acknowledge with grateful hearts the many signal favors of Almighty God."[38]

In his designation of the public holiday which came to be called Thanksgiving, President Washington said,

---

34   James Q Wilson, *American Government, Brief Edition* (Lexington Mass: D. C. Heath, 1987) p. 60

35   Paul Johnson, *A History of the American People* (New York: HarperCollins, 1997) p. 209

36   Paul Johnson, *A History of the American People* (New York: HarperCollins, 1997), p 207

37   Paul Johnson, *A History of the American People* (New York: HarperCollins, 1997), p 207

38   Paul Johnson, *A History of the American People* (New York: HarperCollins, 1997), p 209

It is the duty of all nations to acknowledge the providence of Almighty God, to obey his will, to be grateful for His mercy, to implore His protection and favor… That great and glorious Being who is the beneficent author of all good that was, that is, or that will ever be, that we may then unite in rendering to Him our sincere and humble thanks for His kind care and protection of the people.[39]

Based on their own writings and actions, those who wrote and passed the First Amendment did not see it completely separating church and state. Instead, they saw it as prohibiting the establishment of a national religion. Not only was this the view of the founding fathers, but it has also been the country's view for most of its history.

However, as the twentieth century progressed, the view among many of the educated elite turned increasingly against religion. As historian Edward Purcell noted, religion came to be seen "as the preeminent symbol of everything that was bad in human society."[40]

Many of these elites believed that social improvement would be possible only if religion could be contained, its influence restricted, and society governed on the principles of science and reason.

This negative view of religion vastly differed from that of the founding fathers, who saw it as so important and vital to society that they wrote the First Amendment, mentioning religion first to ensure its protection and freedom. Nor was the founding fathers' view of religion some afterthought; it was an integral part of their political philosophy.

All societies need some boundaries to set the limits of acceptable human behavior. Those boundaries can come from the government or religion; the more they come from one, the less they need to come from the other. A strong and vibrant religion would reduce the need

---

39   Paul Johnson, *A History of the American People* (New York: HarperCollins, 1997), p 209

40   *The Oxford Companion to the Supreme Court of the United States,* s.v. *Religion* ed. Kermit L. Hall (New York, Oxford University Press, 1992) p. 719

for government and thus reduce the chance that the government would become oppressive and tyrannical.

However, a single dominant religion could be just as oppressive as the government, so they passed the First Amendment to ensure that there would be no established religion.

Given this, it should be no surprise that today, those who push the strongest for a strict separation of church and state often advocate for a much larger and more expansive role for government.

Since judges are among the elites, many adopted this new view of religion. As a result, in 1947, the Supreme Court, in *Everson v. Board of Education*, effectively rewrote the First Amendment. The court reinterpreted its meaning from the understanding for 150 years to the new understanding centered around the phrase "separation of church and state."

> With *Everson*, the Supreme Court clearly signaled that the de facto establishment would be abandoned as a guide to church-state relations... The de facto establishment was built on the premise that religion is essential to civilized society.[41]

So where did the court, particularly Hugo Black, writing for the majority, get the phrase "separation of church and state?"

In 1802, Thomas Jefferson wrote a letter to a Baptist group in Danbury, Connecticut. These Baptists had supported Jefferson in a dispute with some mutual political opponents during the presidential election in which Jefferson was a candidate. He responded by writing:

> I contemplate with solemn reverence that act of the whole American people which declared that their legislature should "make no law respecting an establishment of religion, or prohibiting the free exercise thereof," thus building a wall of separation between Church and State.[42]

---

41 *The Oxford Companion to the Supreme Court of the United States*, s.v. *Religion* ed. Kermit L. Hall (New York, Oxford University Press, 1992) p. 719
42 Thomas Jefferson, *To Messrs. Nehemiah Dodge and Others, a Committee of the Danbury Baptist Association in the State of Connecticut, 1802* in Thomas Jefferson, *Writings*

Jefferson was saying that the institutions of the State, his opponents in Connecticut, and the institutions of the church, his supporters, the Danbury Baptists, must be kept apart. He was supporting the Baptists, not seeking to limit them. As John Wilson and Donald Drakeman wrote in their book *Church and State in American History*,

> the letter is a wholly conventional response, and might question whether it provides a likely foundation for the "wall of separation" it allegedly supports.[43]

With the First Amendment, the framers tried to protect against establishing a national religion. This religion could then use its favored position to oppress, restrict, or even eliminate the influence of others. Its primary purpose was to protect the people's right to practice religion.

Since 1947, people began seeing the separation between government and religion as the "wall of separation" mentioned by Jefferson. With this new view, where religion was once good, something so vital that it had to be protected, now many see it as dangerous, something against which we must protect.

This conflict is not just an abstract legal dispute. The idea that religion is somehow a dangerous holdover from the superstitious past forms the backdrop of much of the rejection of religion today.

More importantly, this view is behind the reinterpretation of the First Amendment, coming from many general misconceptions and errors about religion and Christianity, in particular. We will address many of these in this book.

To understand some of the problems of this new view, consider the question: If we must separate everything religious from government functions, what is religion? After all, if we are to exclude something successfully, we must first know what we should exclude.

---

43   John Wilson and Donald Drakeman ed, *Church and State in American History* (Boston Mass: Beacon Press, 1987) p. 78

More importantly, is a complete separation even possible? Is religion something "private and unconnected to government and other institutions of public life"[44] so it can be neatly blocked off? Is it something we do only in a place of worship at particular times that does not affect the rest of our lives?

What is Religion?

What, then, is religion? Philosophers and academicians have long struggled to come up with a definition of religion that includes all its various forms. As John H Hick, author of the book *Philosophy of Religion,* wrote,

> The nature of religion is a vast and complex subject that can be approached from a bewildering variety of viewpoints… As a result there are a great variety of anthropological, sociological, psychological, naturalistic, and religious theories, of the nature of religion. There is, consequently, no universally accepted definition of religion, and quite possibly there never will be.[45]

You can see the difficulty in defining religion with the various terms used in the attempt. Many terms are themselves decidedly religious. In their book *Living Issues in Philosophy,* Harold Titus, Marilyn Smith, and Richard Nolan had this to say concerning a definition of religion,

> Although we may agree that there is no universally accepted definition of religion, it can be granted that throughout history humanity has exhibited a sense of the sacred and that religion falls under the category of the sacred.[46]

---

44   *The Oxford Companion to the Supreme Court of the United States,* s.v. *Religion* ed. Kermit L. Hall (New York, Oxford University Press, 1992) p. 719

45   John H Hick, *Philosophy of Religion* (Englewood Cliffs: Prentice-Hall, 1973) p. 3

46   Harold Titus et al., *Living Issues in Philosophy* (New York: D.Van Nostrand Company, 1979) p. 351

In his text Exploring Religion, Roger Schmidt defines religion as "seeking and responding to what is experienced as holy."[47]

While these definitions may satisfy some, they tend to be somewhat circular, for they attempt to define religion in terms of what is religious. As such, they are unworkable in any practical sense. One could just as easily ask what is sacred or holy. These definitions are, in reality, sidestepping the issue.

At the time of the First Amendment, religion seemed clear. The time and place in which the founding fathers lived was, for the most part, dominated by Christianity. There were, of course, Jews, and they would have been somewhat familiar with Islam. However, the religions of India and China, along with the native Americans, were so little known, much less understood, that they were not a factor in their understanding of religion. Since Christianity, Judaism, and Islam are all religions centered on a belief in God, the founding fathers saw religion mainly in these terms.

This view of religion remains the most common definition in the United States and could be called the *god-based* definition. In other words, the God you believe in determines your religion. Jews, in a religious sense, are Jews because they believe in and worship Yahweh. Christians see God as the Trinity of Father, Son, and Holy Spirit, and Muslims worship Allah. If you don't believe in God, then by this definition, you are not religious.

While satisfactory for Western religions, the god-based definition is grossly inadequate considering the vast array of religious beliefs. With its 300 million gods and diversity of allegiances, Hinduism still fits into the god-based definition of religion, but not very well.

When we begin to examine the other Eastern religions, this Western definition fails miserably. Buddhism does not even consider the question of God important enough to have taken a stand on it one way or the other. Thus, many Buddhists do not believe in

---

47   Roger Schmidt, *Exploring Religion* (Belmont: Wadsworth Inc, 1980) p. 19

God, and many who do don't think God plays any significant role in human affairs.

Buddhism is, in effect, an agnostic[48] religion. If we adhere to a god-based definition, Buddhism would not be a religion. This is clearly not the case. Buddhism is a religion. So, something is wrong with the god-based definition.

Then, there are the vast varieties of more modern religious beliefs. These do not fit any clear category and come under the general heading of New Age beliefs. These include the worship of nature, Mother Earth or Gaia, reincarnation, channeling, various forms of "connecting with the higher self," Wicca, Witchcraft and other forms of Paganism, Scientology, and Transcendental Meditation, to name a few.

Many in these New Age beliefs don't consider themselves religious because they don't believe in God. In fact, they often criticize "religious beliefs" in general as being superstitious and backward. At the same time, they see their views as modern and scientific.

Still, any objective analysis of these views would consider them religious, even though some lack a belief in a god. So clearly, we cannot limit a definition of religion simply to a belief in god.

Another definition is that religion is how people explained the world before the advent of modern science. This definition is somewhat self-serving for those who claim not to believe in any religion. It basically says that religions are what other people believe in; my beliefs come from science.

This definition implies that religion provides an inadequate view of the world. Religion was tenable and practical only until modern science could come along and discover the truth. This view is not a definition of religion but a statement of belief about religion. Karl Marx's famous definition of religion falls into this category:

---

48   An agnostic is one who does not know whether or not god exists. An atheist is one who believes that god does not exist.

> Religion is the sigh of the oppressed creature, the heart of a heartless world, and the soul of the soulless condition. It is the opium of the people.[49]

Any actual definition cannot contain statements that pass judgment on religion while attempting to define it.

The Nature of Religion

Looking at all religions, whether Western religions like Christianity, Eastern religions like Confucianism, shamanistic religions like those of Indigenous peoples, or the mixtures of beliefs found in the New Age Movement, we see that they all have the same essential purpose. This purpose is to help people relate to the world around them in a very fundamental way.

Religions provide a framework for understanding reality and our place in it. While all religions approach and explain the reality around us in differing ways, what they have in common is that they provide the believer with a framework for understanding what they experience. The understanding that religion provides goes beyond just the functional understanding provided by science. The understanding provided by religion deals more with issues of meaning and significance, or lack thereof.

A key point about these frameworks is that they have starting assumptions.[50] These assumptions are fundamental and form the foundation of our view of reality.

Christianity, for example, sees people as creatures with a dual nature: physical and spiritual. The spiritual nature was created in the image of God but is corrupted by sin. Secularism[51] sees no

49 Karl Marx, *Early Writings* trans and ed by T.B. Bottomore (London: Watts, 1963), pp. 43-44

50 The term assumption here should not be taken negatively. While it is probably true that most people simply accept their framework as true without thinking very much about it; that is not what is in view here. Rather it is that these are fundamental starting points in how we view reality.

51 The term 'Secularism' is used here in a broad and generic sense to refer to the various systems of thought that reject either explicitly or implicitly

dualism in human nature and views humans as an advanced form of animal life.

Neither of these positions can be absolutely proven. The Christian cannot prove that there is a spiritual nature, and the secularist cannot prove that the physical nature is all there is. In the final analysis, both positions must rely on faith to some degree. Once accepted, these positions become foundational in understanding everything from our place in the universe to our moral values.

Therefore, one viable way to view religion is that religion is a fundamental and ultimately unprovable set of beliefs that provide a basis for understanding reality.

In this worldview definition of religion, Muslims see Allah, the God of Islam, as central to existence. The individual's primary goal is to please Allah to preserve their soul. Buddhism's primary goal is not to preserve the individual but to realize that "an individual" is an illusion.

Some who worship nature see all of life as connected by some life force, and the individual's goal is to live in harmony with nature. Secularism considers the individual as the product of natural processes, with no purpose or meaning other than that which the individual may provide.

All of these views are fundamentally different ways of approaching reality. All have, at their core, assumptions that followers cannot prove; all are religious.

The beliefs that make up a religious point of view deal with our fundamental conceptions of the world around us. They ultimately affect how we relate to the world. This view is similar to the protestant theologian Paul Tillich's definition of religion as *"ultimate concern."* Some fundamentally religious questions are:

Is the world around us real, or is it just an illusion?
Is there a supernatural?
Is there a God?

the idea that there is a supernatural component to reality, such as atheism, agnosticism, materialism, etc.

What is human nature?

Do we have free will?

Do good and evil exist?

Is there such a thing as morality?

The answers to these questions will often lead to other questions. If you say there is a God, the question becomes: What is our relationship with God?

This is not a restrictive view of religion. Religions can and do involve much more than just a view of reality. They can include rituals and practices of many types and varieties. Although very common, rituals are not required.

Some people believe religion is so personal it can only be expressed privately between the individual and their god(s). Some in the New Age Movement have drawn their beliefs from so many sources that they, in effect, have a customized one-person religion. Rituals, or any other form of organized worship, may have no place in their religions. It would be difficult to show that these people are less religious simply because they do not participate in organized rituals or express their religion outwardly so that others can see.

On the other hand, many groups and institutions we do not consider religious also have rituals and practices. While a religious wedding obviously has rituals, civil weddings share many of the same rituals, such as exchanging rings.

Education has the ritual of graduation to commemorate academic advancement. In government, there is the swearing-in ceremony when a president or other elected official takes office. Does the fact that we have rituals in these and many other groups and institutions make them religious?

Religions are not simply any set of beliefs. To use a somewhat extreme example, a belief that a Porsche 944 is a better car than a Porsche 911 would not be a religious belief. At least for most people, cars do not affect our fundamental view of reality.

On the other hand, whether the universe was created is a religious question. Whether one answers, 'Yes, God created the universe' or 'No, it came about by chance governed by the laws of nature,' the question is still religious in nature.

Some claim that only the first answer to this question is religious. In contrast, the second answer is not religious but scientific. However, there are several problems with this claim. The first would be on what basis would one make such a distinction? Because one deals with god and the other doesn't? As we have already seen, god is insufficient to define religion.

The flip side of this argument would be claiming that one deals with science and the other doesn't. The problem here is that currently, as detailed in the first volume of this series, no scientific theory accounts for the universe's origin on a purely natural basis. There are also serious fundamental problems with finding one. In addition, there is considerable scientific evidence against the theory that everything occurred simply by chance, and in favor of the idea, some intelligent design was involved.

A critical problem with such fundamental questions is they are tightly integrated with the assumptions we make as part of our worldview. As such, the usual dividing lines between scientific and religious answers break down with such questions.

For example, an essential aspect of most scientific theories is their ability to test through repeatable experiments. The theory of gravity can and has been tested many times by dropping various objects in controlled experiments. However, the universe's origin was a one-time event that does not lend itself to testing and repeatability.

As we examined in the first book in this series, all current theories of the origin are incomplete. They all suffer from the problem of the initial condition. How did the process start in the first place? They need something to start the process. If someday scientists come up with a theory that might explain the creation of the universe in a way that does not require a creator, how could this theory be tested?

Is having faith that someday science will figure it out really that different from having faith in God?

Suppose two people accept the scientific theory of the Big Bang, one believing it happened naturally for some unknown reason, the other that God caused it. Is it reasonable to say one is scientific and the other is religious? Ultimately, both answers address the same fundamental question. Both have unprovable assumptions, and thus both are religious to some extent.

Finally, an objection to this worldview definition, which honestly does have merit, is to say these are not actually religious questions but philosophical. However, the objection itself somewhat demonstrates the issue we are dealing with in this chapter.

When looking at such fundamental questions, the usual distinctions between science, religion, or philosophy, for that matter, tend to break down. Even if we were to conclude these were not religious but philosophical questions, it would not fundamentally change the point here. The various answers to these questions share the same qualities; it would simply change the label by which we refer to those qualities.

Religion and the Person

We can draw certain conclusions if we accept this worldview definition of religion. The first is that there is no such thing as a non-religious person. Since everyone has answers of one sort or another to these fundamental questions of origins, meaning, and significance, everyone has some kind of religion. They may not have a traditional religion or attend any church or worship service. They may not believe in any God, but they have a religion.

Because of this, many do not like this definition. Some people are adamant that their worldview cannot be religious because it is not based on faith. Others see religion as a fundamentally inferior way of thinking. For them, labeling something as "*religious*" is effectively the same as saying it is false.

In contrast, they see their views as based only on facts and reason. If you cannot prove it, then they will not believe it. But again, this is not only self-serving but is, at best, more a statement of belief about traditional religions than a definition.

Still, there is a more fundamental problem with this claim. No worldview is based entirely only on "facts and reason." Facts by themselves are meaningless. They must have a framework that ties them together before becoming meaningful.

The number two may be a fact, but what does it mean? By itself, it is meaningless. Given a context, such as how many dollars you owe me, suddenly, two becomes meaningful. If, on the other hand, two is how many dollars I owe you, it could take on even more meaning!

In short, we need a framework or context before facts become meaningful. Change the context, and you can significantly change the meaning. It is a fact that, at the equator, the sun rises in the east in the morning. However, this fact means something different in the Ptolemaic system (earth-centric universe) than the Copernican system (sun-centric solar system). When you see the sun rising, is it really rising, or is this the result of the earth spinning?

The same can be said for reason. Reason is simply a tool and must operate within some framework, in this case, a series of assumptions about the nature of the world around us.

A sociologist and a psychologist could take the same facts and, using reason, might reach entirely different conclusions concerning people's actions. It is not so much that one is more scientific than the other; instead, they start with different assumptions through which they view these facts.

This concept of a mental framework is a central theme of James Burke's book and PBS television series, *The Day the Universe Changed*. Burke points out that discoveries have fundamentally altered how we view the world around us at certain times in our history. It is not so much that the facts changed, but our viewing of them. According to Burke:

> At different times in the past, reality was observed differ-
> ently. Different societies coexisting in the modern world have
> different structures of reality... Even at the individual level,
> perceptions of reality are unique and autonomous. Each one
> of us has his own mental structure of the world by which
> he may recognize new experience. In a world today so full
> of new experiences, this ability is necessary for survival. But
> by definition, the structure also provides the user with hy-
> potheses about events before they are experienced. The events
> then fit the hypothesis, or are rejected as being unrecognizable
> and without meaning. Without the structure, in other words,
> there can be no reality.

The structure is, in many ways, truly more important than, and gives meaning to, the facts. So, to claim that one only relies on facts and reason completely ignores what Burke calls our "own mental structure" in which these operate.[52]

Tools of Knowledge

There is a distinction between tools of knowledge and religions. Tools of knowledge are just that, tools that we use to help us learn. Science is one such tool. We can use science to learn about the physical world around us. Science, however, is not perfect and does have its problems. As James Burke put it, science

> is not what it appears to be. It is not objective and impar-
> tial, since every observation it makes of nature is impregnated
> with theory. Nature is so complex and so random that it can
> only be approached with a systematic tool that presuppos-
> es certain facts about it. Without such a pattern it would be
> impossible to find an answer to questions even as simple as
> "What am I looking at?"[53]

---

52 James Burke, *The Day the Universe Changed* (Boston: Little Brown and
Co, 1985) pp. 307-8
53 Burke, *Day*, p. 336

The following example illustrates the problem with tools. Suppose a researcher plots the raw data for a particular issue, getting the arrangement of dots shown in Figure 2.1. Without some theory, these would seem simply a random collection of dots.

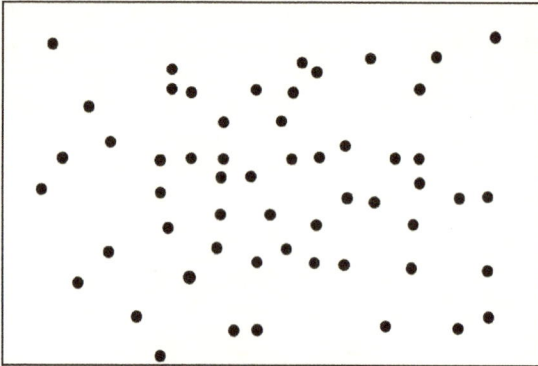

Figure 2.1

Now, someone trying to come up with a theory to explain the arrangement of these dots might theorize that these dots form some arrangement based on straight lines and 90-degree angles. Curved lines and angles other than 90 degrees are not allowed.

In order to test this "Square" theory, they developed tools to measure straight lines and 90-degree angles. When they apply these tools to the raw data, they find that, as seen in Figure 2.2, most of the dots fall into just such an arrangement.

Very few theories perfectly explain all of the available data. So, for this example, we assume there are limits on the resulting squares and rectangle size. The Square theory cannot currently explain all dots. Still, the Square theory explains enough of the dots to make it seem plausible or at least on the right track.

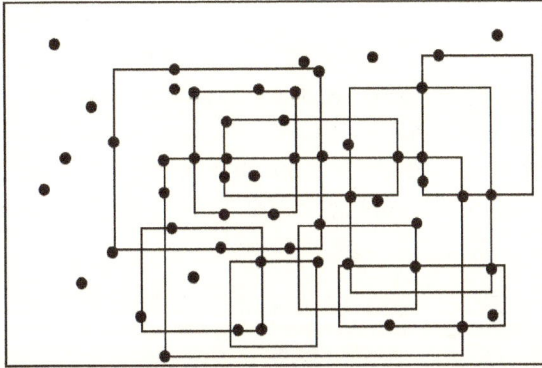

Figure 2.2

Yet not all are convinced. Others believe the explanation is in curves rather than straight lines and angles. No straight lines or angles are allowed.

To test this "Circle" theory, supporters develop tools that search for curved lines, and like the supporters of the Square theory, they also find that their Circle theory accounts for most, but not all, of the dots, as is seen in Figure 2.3

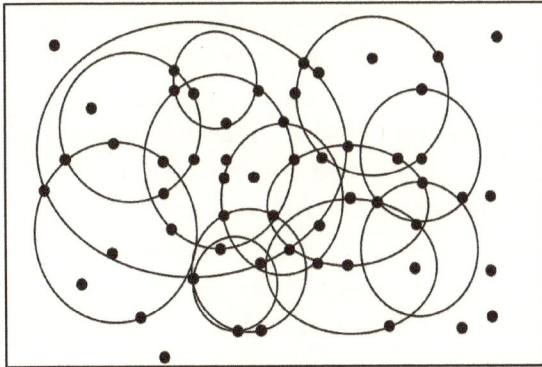

Figure 2.3

Both sides can claim to have a theory that explains the arrangement of the dots and that the evidence supports them. Both could argue that they do not see much support for the other camp's theory as the tools they use are ill-equipped to find it.

As Figure 2.4 shows, both theories account for most dots. Both approaches can explain some dots not explained by the other, and there are some dots for which neither theory can account. In short, which theory one accepts depends heavily on the assumptions one makes and, thus, the tools chosen.

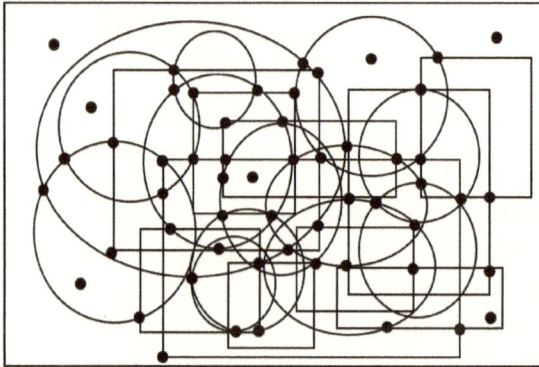

Figure 2.4

When dealing with the usual questions of scientific inquiry, this is not too much of a problem. However, there are notable examples in the history of science where scientists rejected a new theory because it did not fit the established scientific framework. Only later, once the old framework had broken down, was it accepted. This is precisely what happened to Alfred Lothar Wegener.

Wegener was a German meteorologist at the beginning of the twentieth century and co-developer of the Wegener-Bergeron-Findeisen procedure used to study ice crystals. But his interest went beyond meteorology.

One day, while looking at a map of the world, he was suddenly struck by how the coastline of South America seemed to match the coastline of Africa. It was as if they had at one time been together. Intrigued, Wegener began to investigate the idea further.

Looking at a wide range of research, including geology, paleontology, and biology, he began to find a lot of evidence to support his theory. Not only did the coastlines seem to match, but so did the mountain ranges, mineral deposits, and fossils; all seemed to line up when you put the continents together.

After a while, Wegener gathered enough detailed evidence to show how the continents had been connected into one giant supercontinent. He also developed an idea of how and when they broke up to be in their current positions.

As with many scientific theories, Wegener was not the first to consider the idea, but he was the first to gather all the evidence and publish it in 1915 in *The Origin of the Continents and Oceans.*

Today, the theories of Wegener concerning what he called "continental displacement" are taught as continental drift and are seen as fundamental to our understanding of the geological development of the planet. At the time he published them, however, they were not so well received.

While a few were at least open to Wegener's theory and the evidence he had amassed to support it, most were downright hostile.

"Utter, damned rot!" said the president of the American Philosophical Society. "If we are to believe this hypothesis we must forget everything we learned in the last seventy years and start all over again," remarked Thomas Chamberlin, a towering figure in American geology, on hearing of Wegener speak in New York in 1923. "Anyone who valued his reputation for scientific sanity," said a British geologist, at the same time, when Wegener's ideas were being given wide airing, "would never dare support such a theory."[54]

Not only was Wegener's theory rejected, but he was also denounced and scorned. His evidence written off as mere fantasy.

And so Wegner was pushed out into the cold, like a querulous customer in a barroom of rowdies. Not a single German

54 Simon Winchester, *Krakatoa, The Day the World Exploded August 27, 1883* (New York: Harper Collins, 2003) p. 74

university would give him the professorship that his otherwise impeccable pedigree deserved; it was left to the University of Graz, in Austria, to offer him only the chair in meteorology. He was obliged to stand away from the geology that was the business of others.

Sadly, it was thirty years after Wegener's death before the weight of the evidence in favor of Wegener's theory became so overwhelming that scientists could no longer ignore it. Wegener was finally vindicated.[55]

Wegener's problem was not a lack of evidence. In fact, not only is his theory now readily accepted, but it is also taught using much of the same evidence as Wegener's.

The real problem was that Wegener's theory did not fit the established scientific understanding of his day. As Chamberlin noted, if true, geologists would have to "start all over again." It was heresy, and the scientific community did what it could to suppress it.

Science is not a perfect tool, nor is it free from problems.[56] If Wegner had these problems with a scientific question in geology, one could imagine the problems when dealing with more fundamental questions, questions where science and religion overlap, such as the universe's origin.

One example of this is in the Creation/Evolution debate.[57] Life is very diverse and complex. Evolution theory claims that all life is ultimately related, with new species evolving from other species back to a common origin.

On the other hand, many creationists see different kinds of life created specially by God. All life is not ultimately related. As paleontologist Kurt P. Wise points out,

---

55   Winchester, *Krakatoa*, p. 75

56   One might argue that the problem is not with science but with scientists, but the end result would be the same.

57   As detailed in the first volume of this series, *Evidence for the Bible*, there are Christians on both sides of this issue. The point here is not which side is right, but the assumptions they make and the tools they use.

Christianity and Secularism

Since evolutionary theory suggests all organisms are ultimately related to one another and all biologic structure is derived from other biologic structure, evolutionists don't believe there is any such thing as true discontinuity. Evolutionists did not, therefore, develop a tool for identifying discontinuity. Their classification tools are completely blind to it. Even if the world was full of discontinuity (as young-age creationism suggests), evolutionists would not be able to see it.

Like the Square and Circle theories of the earlier example, evolutionists develop tools to show evolution and then use those tools to find evidence. Meanwhile, young earth creationists developed tools to show creation and, likewise, find evidence for it.[58]

A more significant problem arises if one tries to make science into a complete description of all reality. At that point, the tool becomes a religion.

Science as a tool works well for describing and learning about the natural world, but only the natural world. It tells us little or nothing about the possible existence of a reality beyond the natural, which is generally referred to as the supernatural. Science has its limitations.

A clear example of the line between a tool and a religion can be seen in Carl Sagan's PBS television series and accompanying book, *COSMOS*. In the first episode, Sagan described how Eratosthenes discovered that the earth was a sphere. This is science. These are facts about the physical world that one can examine, test, and confirm.

At the program's start, however, Sagan begins with the statement, "The Cosmos is all that is or ever was or ever will be."[59] This statement is not open to examination or testing. It is a statement not of science but of religion.

To see this, consider the following. Sagan's statement implies that the natural universe, the cosmos, is all reality, "is all that is or

---

58 Kurt Wise, *Faith Form and Time* (B&H Publishing Group, 2002) p 263 Note 11

59 Carl Sagan, *COSMOS* (New York: Random House, 1980) p. 4

ever was or ever will be." Science, which studies the natural world, has no limitations and is the study of reality.

If this is true, we rule out the possibility that God exists. How could a tool limited to learning about the natural world ever discover the creator of the natural world? At best, the only evidence that science could provide for the existence of God would be indirect. Since we cannot indirectly provide the evidence required to show the existence of God to a person with such a worldview, the existence of God is ruled out.

Notice that no evidence, either pro or con, is needed to reach this conclusion. The rejection of the existence of God is simply a logical outcome of the fundamental assumption that sees science as the explanation for *all* of reality. It boils down to the fact that if science cannot explain God, God must not exist. As a fundamental and ultimately unprovable belief that provides a basis for understanding reality, it is a statement of religion.

Some have tried to avoid this problem by claiming they only accept that science describes all of reality until someone can prove it does not. This is sophistry.

What would be the basis for this proof? If it is not science, then science is not the final judge of reality as is being claimed. If it is scientific proof, then the claim becomes tautological.

Science is the final judge of reality, except where science shows that science does not apply. Not only is this circular, but it also raises the question of how science can show that science does not apply?

As such, even those claiming their view of reality comes only from facts and reason still must make assumptions. Accepting these assumptions has a component of faith, and even they have a religion.

Impossibility of Absolute Proof

The second conclusion we can draw from a worldview definition of religion is that the concept of absolute proof has no real meaning when comparing differing religions. This is because concepts of proof are very closely related to the evaluation of evidence.

A distinction needs to be made here between proof and evidence. When we state that we cannot absolutely prove a particular position and, therefore, one must, to some degree, have faith, it does not mean that there is no evidence for that position.

Faith is not necessarily blind and unsupported by evidence, nor is it, as H. L. Mencken described it, "an illogical belief in the occurrence of the improbable."[60] If this were true, this would be a very short book, as this is a book about evidence. Faith can be supported by evidence.[61]

To say that we cannot absolutely prove that the universe started in a tremendous explosion called the Big Bang, which we cannot, does not mean that there is no evidence to support this theory. There is a great deal of evidence to support the Big Bang theory.

While strong enough to convince the scientific community, this evidence does not prove that the Big Bang occurred. Some faith is required to believe in the Big Bang. It may not need very much, but it does require some.

When discussing religion, a significant problem is that our evaluation of evidence is inseparable from our worldview, thus our religion. This problem is why the claims made by other religions sometimes seem beyond belief. People from other religions can believe things that might seem absurd and ludicrous because their fundamental assumptions and perceptions of reality are different.

This issue is the problem with atheists who constantly demand proof that God exists. The problem is not a lack of evidence. As we will see in later chapters, there is considerable evidence to support the existence of God.

The real problem is that, for atheists, no evidence will ever be sufficient to constitute proof. Atheists will continually reinterpret any evidence put forth to fit their worldview in a naturalistic way

60   H. L. Mencken, *Prejudices, Third Series*, ch 14
61   For a more complete discussion of the concepts of faith, reason, proof and evidence and their interrelations, See Volume III of this series, *Faith and Reason*.

that does not demand the existence of God. As James Burke put it in the earlier passage, "The events then fit the hypothesis, or are rejected as being unrecognizable and without meaning."[62]

In many respects, it is the same problem that Wegner faced with the geologist of his day. Atheists reject the evidence for creation and intelligent design, as well as the evidence presented in this book and the other books in this series. It does not fit their worldview, so they write it off as meaningless. In the atheist's view of reality, there is no room for a god; therefore, God cannot exist, and you cannot have evidence for something that does not exist.

This issue is also why it is useless to say, as some agnostics claim, that their views are not religious but simply common sense. The problem with this view is that what is common sense from one point of view could be considered ridiculous from another. What is common sense depends on our worldview.

These problems do not mean any discussion concerning opposing religious views is meaningless. As we have already seen, "faith" does not mean "in spite of the evidence." Discussing and contrasting the evidence for different religions without demanding absolute proof is possible.

Some have problems with the idea that there is no absolute proof.[63] Surely, we can prove that the things we can see and touch at least exist simply by seeing and touching them.

George Berkeley pointed out the problems with such claims in the eighteenth century. Attempting to stem the rise of the belief that the material world is the only thing that exists, Berkeley formulated a view that he hoped would refute it once and for all. In the process, he destroyed the world.

Materialists claimed the material world was the only thing that existed because it was the only thing we could know from our

---

62 Burke, *Day*, p. 307-8

63 Do not confuse the concepts of absolute proof with the concept of absolute truth. While related they are not the same thing. It is very possible to reject the concept of absolute proof, and yet still firmly believe in absolute truth.

senses. It was the only thing that we could touch, see, etc. Berkeley fought materialism by taking their reasoning even further.

Berkeley accepted the materialist claim that existence is limited to what we can directly know and experience. He then pointed out we cannot directly know or experience anything about the material world. When we *see* a chair, table, or anything, we are not directly experiencing the chair or table, even if we assume that the material world exists.

Assuming there was a material world, what we call seeing is light in the form of photons striking the chair and bouncing off. Some of these photons enter our eyes, which convert them into electrical impulses. These impulses travel along the optic nerve to our brains. Once in the brain, the electrical impulses become a perception of the chair. Chair ⇨ photon ⇨ electrical impulses ⇨ perception.

While the eye may directly react to light, our mind only responds to the perceptions created by the electrical impulses it receives. As such, if the materialists are correct, and the only things we can know exist are those we directly experience, the only things we can really know are real are our perceptions. As Berkeley put it,

> It is the mind that frames all that variety of bodies which compose the visible world, any one whereof does not exist longer than it is perceived.[64]

Lord Chesterfield, one of Berkeley's critics, admitted that Berkeley's "arguments are, strictly speaking, unanswerable."[65] When covering Berkeley's views in class, students often recast the problem: "How do we know that we are not living in the Matrix?"

Few would say that Berkeley is correct in claiming that the material world does not exist or that we live in a Matrix-like world. Still, the point here is that if we cannot absolutely prove the existence of the material world we see around us, how could we prove anything?

---

64 Will and Ariel Durant, *The Age of Louis XIV*, (New York, Simon and Schuster, 1963) p. 595
65 Durant, p. 595

Another way to put this is: suppose I believe that nothing exists except me, that everything else is simply a product of my imagination. With some thought, we can show that this worldview is not very tenable. In fact, I have never met anyone who seriously held this position,   which is probably a good thing. After all, if other people were not real, only imagined, why would it matter how you treated them or what you did to them?

Yet, if I did hold this view and were to demand that you absolutely prove that you did exist, you would quickly find it impossible. If for no other reason, it would be impossible because, from my view of reality, you are just an illusion. Why should I believe anything an illusion says or does?

The Importance of Faith

The final conclusion we will draw from the worldview-based definition of religion is that, since it is impossible to talk about absolute proof, all views have a faith component. By faith, we do not mean acceptance *despite* the evidence. Instead, it is an acceptance that goes *beyond* the evidence, and it is an acceptance that leads to some action.

In short, we believe it enough to act on it. The evidence for a particular position may be strong or weak. Yet, when we move beyond the evidence to accept a position such that we make decisions based on it, this is faith. In many cases, faith is required of us; we cannot avoid it.

Most people believe that adults should be held responsible for their actions, provided they are mentally competent. This concept forms the basis for our legal system and social structure.

This belief is why we distinguish in the law between killing a person by accident and deliberately killing them. In the latter case, we believed the person chose to kill, while in the former, they did not.

Still, this concept assumes we have the free will to choose our actions. Yet, we cannot prove we can make choices, and a growing number of scientists reject the concept. To accept free will, we must have faith.

While free will is a problem for everyone, for those claiming only the natural world exists and that there is no supernatural, the existence of free will is especially troublesome. It seems insolvable. As John Searle, professor of philosophy at the University of California, Berkeley, wrote,

> Our conception of ourselves as free agents is fundamental to our self-conception. Now, ideally, I would like to be able to keep both my commonsense conceptions and my scientific beliefs... But when it comes to the question of freedom and determinism, I am – like a lot of other philosophers – unable to reconcile the two.[66]

Before we proceed, let us be clear about what free will means versus determinism. To say that we have free will does not mean we can do anything we want. I cannot, for example, decide to fly by simply flapping my arms and making it so. The question of free will is whether we can make *any* decision or whether everything is determined.

Suppose you are hungry and go to a restaurant with an extensive menu and many things you like to eat. Furthermore, for this example, money and calories are not issues that concern you. Do you have any actual freedom to choose what to eat (free will), or would the choice have been pre-determined by the laws of nature (determinism) such that you had no choice?

Most people would say, of course, they had a choice. In fact, you can probably think of a time when you were in a similar situation and had trouble choosing. Doesn't having trouble choosing imply a choice?

While we all have this clear perception of choice, how does choice happen in a universe governed by natural law? To see the problem, look at how the rest of nature works. Be it the motion

---

66 John Searle, *Minds, Brains, and Science,* (Cambridge, MA, Harvard University Press, 1984) p. 86

of the planets, the formation of snowflakes, or the growth of a plant, the laws of nature determine everything. There is no choice involved. Even when the events are so random as to be unpredictable, there is still no choice.

Drop a series of rocks off the side of a tall mountain and see how they bounce down the steep slope. You will find that you cannot predict precisely where any rock might land.

Each time a rock strikes the side of the mountain or a protruding ledge, it will bounce in a new direction only to hit somewhere else and bounce off in another direction until it finally comes to rest in the valley below. While so complex as to be unpredictable in advance, the result is not one of choice.

At every bounce, the laws of nature determine how the rock falls. From the moment you drop the rock, these laws determine its ultimate landing spot, even though its arrival at that spot is still in the future.

Its exact landing spot depends on exactly how you dropped it, environmental factors such as windspeed, and the shape of the mountain. If all of these factors were precisely the same for every rock you drop, every rock would land in the same place. That's how a universe governed by natural laws works.

The problem of free will is where does our choice come into this. The first response of many to this question is to point out a critical difference between us and the rock: we have a brain. It is our brain that gives us the ability to make choices.

Ok, but then how does the brain make a choice? The brain is a biological organ of 100 billion neurons interconnected by synapses. The brain responds to electrical impulses from the body sent along the nerves and responds in the same way. Biology, chemistry, and physics laws govern how electrical impulses move about the brain at every step.

If we call consciousness the sum total of neurons, synapses, and the electrical impulses moving among them, all governed by natural law, where does free will enter into this? At what point does this transcend natural law to allow for the concept of choice?

Returning to the restaurant example above, your brain would respond to a series of impulses. Impulses from your senses give you a perception of the restaurant, menu, time of day, etc. Impulses from your body give you a perception of being hungry.

These would combine with memories concerning what you liked and disliked and what you have recently had. The laws of nature govern each of these impulses. So, just where would a concept of choice fit?

Besides being far more complex, how would the impulses bouncing around your brain be any different than the rock bouncing down a mountain? It wouldn't. The laws of nature govern both scenarios, so the outcome, possibly unpredictable, will be determined. There would be no room for free will, and the belief that we can choose would be an illusion.

Some argued descriptions, such as the one we have just presented, are missing a critical aspect of the laws of nature. Such depictions assume a Newtonian view of the universe. But now physicists know that Newton's laws are not the whole story. Quantum physics introduces the uncertainty principle, leaving room for choice. But there is still a problem.

It is true that in quantum physics, there are things we cannot determine in quite the same way as with Newton's laws. For example, in Newtonian physics, if you know an object's exact position and velocity and the forces acting on it, you can calculate precisely where that object will be in ten seconds or ten years.

The problem is that in quantum physics, you cannot know both position and velocity beyond a certain degree of accuracy. If you seek to determine the position more precisely, you lose the ability to know the velocity and vice versa. This level of uncertainty in the position and velocity translates into uncertainty about where the object will be in 10 seconds.

While quantum physics does introduce uncertainty, there is a considerable gap between uncertainty and choice. Some speculate that this gap may be filled if scientists can link consciousness to quantum uncertainty. As physicist Brian Greene put it when discussing the problem of free will:

> We might one day find, as some physicists have speculated, that the act of conscious observation is an integral element of quantum mechanics, being the catalyst that coaxes one outcome from the quantum haze to be realized. Personally, I find this extremely unlikely, but I know of no way to rule it out.[67]

That a universe governed by natural law leaves room for such a thing as free will is, at best, speculation.[68] Yet, there is no way to avoid a question as fundamental as this.

One certainly cannot prove that people have some degree of free will. But one must either accept or reject it to interact in the world. While the scientific evidence is against the idea that we have free will, it would be pretty hard to live as if it did not exist. Still, the decision, while possibly based to some extent on evidence, must have a component of faith in the final analysis.

Faith is more than just a feeling or belief; it is a conviction. It is a conviction so firm that we base our lives on it. Often, the conviction is held so firmly it is taken for granted, with disbelief and puzzlement as to why everyone doesn't accept it. "It is clear; why doesn't everyone see it?"

This conclusion will be the hardest to accept for those who take great pride in relying only on facts, science, and reason. To them, the concept of faith is repugnant. However, one can maintain a

---

67 Brian Greene, *The Fabric of the Cosmos* (New York: Knoph, 2004) pp. 456

68 Nor is it at all certain that if physicists were to find that consciousness was an integral part of quantum mechanics that this would be automatically a good thing for atheists or agnostics. After all if as physicist John Wheeler who supports such a role has claimed, "No elementary phenomenon is a phenomenon until it is an observed phenomenon" is correct, who was around to observe the elementary phenomena in the Big Bang?

rejection of faith only by ignoring the fundamental assumptions that everyone must make. We cannot prove these assumptions, so faith plays a role.

In the final analysis, whether one labels it religion, worldview, philosophy, or whatever, at some point, all views of reality involve faith. They are, in that sense, religious.

We are left with a definition of religion as the framework in which each person understands reality. Although there may be evidence for or against a given view, the final decision is one in which faith plays a role.

If someone steadfastly refuses to be included under a definition of religion, then so be it. We have seen that claims of belief based only on reason and facts rest on shaky ground. Although they may not wish to be classified as religious, this does not eliminate the fact that everyone must have some concept of reality and that all concepts of reality fundamentally involve, to some extent, faith. One may wish to use some name other than religion, but as Shakespeare wrote:

> That which we call a rose
> By any other name would smell as sweet.[69]

Religion is an integral part of being human. It is not a question of whether or not to be religious, for everyone has a religion. The real question is which religion is correct.[70]

We cannot hide behind demands for absolute proof but must honestly evaluate the evidence. I am convinced and will attempt to show in the remainder of this book that the claims of Christianity are strongly supported when we assess the evidence with an open mind. Christianity is a faith solidly grounded on facts.

---

69 Shakespeare, *Romeo and Juliet*, I ii 43
70 Often people ask why all the religions of the world can't be correct? This, however, is impossible since different religions make different and contradictory claims (e.g., God does exist - God does not exist). While all religions could be wrong, they cannot all be correct.

2

Is That All There Is?

There are more things in heaven and earth, Horatio,
Than are dreamt of in your philosophy.

(Hamlet)[71]

42

(Deep Thought)[72]

URING THE MIDDLE of the nineteenth century, a great
debate raged over the origin of life. One side, led by the
French bacteriologist Felix-Archimede Pouchet, argued that
life arose spontaneously from non-living matter. The other, led by
Louis Pasteur, said this was impossible; life could only come from
other life. To some, this was just an interesting scientific discussion.
However, it was quite literally a matter upon which thousands,
possibly even millions of lives depended. Perhaps even yours.

During this time, hospitals were a dangerous place to be. Mortality rates for women during childbirth in hospitals could be as
high as 30 percent, mostly from puerperal infection or, as it was
more commonly known, childbed fever.

Mortality rates for surgery ranged between 45 - 50 percent,
again with infection being the primary cause of death. Even a broken bone that pierced the skin was life-threatening. Many doctors

---

71 Shakespeare, *Hamlet*, I v 16
72 This is the answer to the great question of Life the Universe and
Everything as given by the computer Deep Thought. Douglas Adams, *The*
Hitchhiker's Guide to the Galaxy

believed that these infections were an inescapable risk and that they could do nothing to prevent them.

In 1844, Ignaz Semmelweis was a young doctor working in an obstetric clinic in Vienna. Disregarding the objections of his chief physician, he began working on the problem of childbed fever.

His clinic had two wards: one staffed by midwives and the other by medical students. The only other difference between the two wards was that the ward staffed by students had a two to three times higher mortality rate than the one staffed by midwives. This perplexed Semmelweis. In his mind, it should have been the other way around.

One day, a friend of Semmelweis was performing an autopsy on a woman who died of childbed fever when he accidentally cut himself. Before long, the wound became infected, and his friend died.

As a result, Semmelweis began to wonder if the cause of the infection might be something in the body. He knew the students went directly from the autopsy room to the maternity ward. He wondered if they were transferring the disease from the bodies of women who had died to those in the ward.

Semmelweis decided to try an experiment. What would happen if he required the students to wash their hands before each examination? For us today, the results are unsurprising. Still, for Semmelweis, they were amazing. The mortality rate dropped from 18 percent to 1 percent. Over the next few years, mortality in Semmelweis' clinic averaged less than one percent, while other clinics in the area had rates from 10 - 15 percent.

Even with this success, other doctors rejected his research as nonsense. Semmelweis struggled for over twenty years to get doctors to wash their hands. In the end, he failed. In terms of human lives, the cost of that failure was staggering.

For example, the American Civil War began fifteen years after Semmelweis discovered the benefits of doctors washing their hands. During the Civil War, over 600,000 soldiers died, mostly from diseases and infections. Had Semmelweis convinced the medical community, his research could have saved many of these lives.

Finally, his spirit broken, Semmelweis suffered a mental breakdown and was committed to a hospital. It was in the hospital that, ironically, he died of an infection in 1865, the year the Civil War ended.

Pasteur's and Pouchet's little debate on the origin of life directly influenced the rejection of Semmelweis' work. If life arises spontaneously, as most doctors at the time believed, they could do little to prevent infection. Washing your hands between patients could not possibly help because bacteria would appear on any open wound spontaneously.

If, on the other hand, life came only from other life, as Pasteur argued, an infection would never get started if you could keep bacteria away from a wound. Pasteur's position forms the basis for the modern germ theory of disease.

In the same year Semmelweis died, Joseph Lister, a British surgeon, became interested in Pasteur's theories. Lister was concerned about the high death rates following amputations, which approached 50 percent.

When Lister began to apply Pasteur's theories to his practice, the results were once again dramatic. Mortality rates drop to about 15 percent. While the opposition continued, Lister was more fortunate than Semmelweis.

After years of dramatic successes, Lister and Pasteur finally reversed medical opinion. The medical community accepted the germ theory of disease, one of the most important discoveries in the history of medicine.

A significant reason for opposing the germ theory was its dependence on Pasteur's theory that life comes only from other life. Many scientists felt Pasteur's theory had a serious, if not fatal, flaw, which Pouchet and his supporters quickly pointed out.

If life comes only from other life, how did life ever get started in the first place? Spontaneous generation was seen as necessary to explain the very existence of life unless you wanted to resort to supernatural explanations, such as that created by God.

Empirical evidence is the basis for modern science, evidence that the five senses can detect, whether naturally or with mechanical or electronic instruments. As such, scientists automatically reject any supernatural explanation.

While the germ theory itself was not supernaturally based, it contradicted what was, at the time, the only non-supernatural explanation for the origin of life: spontaneous generation. Only after Darwin's theory of evolution sparked an interest in chemical evolution as an explanation for life did doctors finally accept the germ theory.[73] While some scientists may reject the supernatural, their rejection comes not from science but from the philosophical/religious belief that science describes all of reality. Most, but not all, traditional religions accept as an integral part of life the concept that there is more to existence than that which the five senses can detect. Existence does not end with the natural world. Any reality beyond the natural, beyond what the five senses can detect, is referred to as the supernatural.[74]

A Question of Proof

Does the supernatural exist? Any discussion between the opposing points of view is challenging because of the fundamental nature of the question. A belief in or rejection of the supernatural goes to the foundation of our concepts of reality.

Many atheists and agnostics demand proof of the existence of the supernatural before they will accept it. As we pointed out in the last chapter, absolute proof is impossible. Not only is absolute proof impossible, but the existence of the supernatural is so fun-

73 The theory of chemical evolution of life is not much better than spontaneous generation. For a discussion see *Evidence for the Bible*, Consider Christianity Series, Volume 1, Chapter 4.

74 There are some additional issues concerning the use of the terms 'natural' and 'supernatural' when it comes to science and creation. For a discussion see *Evidence for the Bible, Consider Christianity Series, Volume 1*, Chapter 5.

damental that virtually any proof is difficult, especially given the subjective nature of evidence.[75]

Discussions concerning the supernatural often result in a dispute over who should prove what. Do those who accept the existence of the supernatural need to prove that it exists, or is it the skeptic's responsibility to prove that it does not?

The skeptic cannot prove that the supernatural does not exist. In almost all practical circumstances, it is impossible to prove a negative. For instance, it is impossible to prove that little green men do not live on the Moon. This is because, for every line of evidence, there would always be a way around it.

The argument that we have never seen these little green men is easily handled by saying that we have not seen them because they are hiding. They take great precautions to keep from being detected. If one cannot disprove such a silly proposition, one could never hope to prove that the supernatural does not exist.

Since it is impossible for the skeptic to prove that the supernatural does not exist, does the believer have the burden of proof that it does? At first glance, this might seem reasonable. When considering the argument that little green men live on the moon, the burden of proof rests with those who claim they do. Likewise, the skeptic argues that those who believe in the supernatural must provide proof of its existence.

This argument only seems reasonable until one considers how a believer might do so. The skeptic will only accept empirical evidence. But the supernatural is that part of reality that empirical means cannot detect. How can the believer give empirical evidence for the existence of the supernatural that would be acceptable to the skeptic? They cannot, so empirical proof for the existence of the supernatural is also impossible.

---

75 In such discussions, proof is simply the level of evidence required to accept something as true and there is no fixed objective standard for how much evidence this requires. It varies from person to person, and even from issue to issue. Thus it is subjective.

This conundrum raises the question: If you can't prove that the supernatural exists, why believe it does? How can you know that the supernatural exists?

Part of the solution is the realization this is not an issue of who needs to prove what to whom. Our concepts of proof are so intertwined with our fundamental views of reality that the demands for proof in such cases become virtually meaningless.

Such demands are little more than a defense mechanism for those who make them. They also have a significant problem with circular reasoning, as the proof demanded would depend on their worldview. This worldview rejects the very thing for which they require proof.

Those making such claims effectively say, 'I can ignore your position if you can't give me proof.' This is why, for example, atheists and agnostics so frequently claim there is no evidence for the existence of God.

Such claims do not come from a lack of evidence, for there is a great deal. Instead, these claims come from the false notion that they can ignore anything that does not constitute proof by their standards. It does not exist.[76]

Rather than asking which side should prove or disprove something, a better approach is to realize that both sides have different and competing views of reality. Advocates for either view cannot prove theirs is correct, and both views require, to some extent, faith.

All such foundational views have pros and cons that must be weighed and considered. As a result, we need to ask a somewhat different question: which worldview better explains reality? The

---

76 This is also a good example of the subjective nature of proof, for while agnostics and atheists may have a very high, and in reality impossible, standard of proof for things that do not fit their worldview such as the existence of the supernatural or God, they are more than willing to except things that do fit their worldview, sometimes even when the evidence is against what they believe, a case in point being free will as discussed in the last chapter.

advantage of this question is it focuses on the evidence rather than some arbitrary and subjective standards of proof.

The determined skeptic will never accept the existence of the supernatural. They see their position as correct by default and then demand those with different beliefs meet some safely unattainable level of proof or be rejected.

Still, there is considerable evidence to support a belief in the supernatural. This evidence is not empirical but is experiential, that which comes from experience, historical, and philosophical.

We are, for the most part, tied to the physical world around us. Since the rise of modern scientific thought, our concepts of proof have also been increasingly connected to the natural world. One of the most fundamental concepts of science is the demand for tests and verification.

Because of this, personal experience plays a minimal role in science. We must test our experiences. When dealing with the physical world, this causes few problems. It usually is not too difficult to set up a test that others can repeat and verify.

When we are dealing with the supernatural, this isn't easy. When tests are done that point to some supernatural activity, this rarely causes the skeptic to accept the existence of the supernatural. Often, it is just written off or ignored.

A case in point is the experiments that show the benefits of prayer on healing. In one double-blind study on coronary care patients, those being prayed for did better in 21 of 26 monitored categories than those who were not.[77]

When not just ignoring supernatural explanations, skeptics suggest new theories as a natural explanation. This allows them to classify the supposed supernatural activity as a natural phenomenon. Often, evidence is not necessary, only the mere suggestion is

---

77 Gary R. Habermas, *Did Jesus Perform Miracles?* In *Jesus under Fire*, ed Michael J Wilkins, J. P. Morland, (Grand Rapids, MI, Zondervan, 1995) p. 132-3

enough. As a result, rather than evidence for the supernatural, it becomes evidence that it does not exist.

For some, believing something we cannot prove empirically might be disturbing. Still, we all accept things we cannot prove empirically; we often take them for granted.

The existence of love is virtually universally accepted and un-questioned. Can we empirically show that love does exist? Can we measure it in the laboratory? No. Still, we accepted love as fact based on the evidence of human experience. Just because we cannot empirically prove that love exists did not cause much concern or lead some to reject it until recently. Recently, some deny the existence of love, claiming it is an illusion of biochemistry. As a character in the movie *Down To You* put it,

> "Love is a hoax. Our emotions are
> all provoked by chemical reactions.
> It creates this euphoria
> that makes you stupid.
> It's all biochemistry. Trust me.
> It was my major.
> I'm afraid it's true, Al.
> All romantics are simply addicts."

Secularism

The movement of modern society away from a belief in the supernatural generally comes under the heading of secularization.[78] The word secular means pertaining to this world or worldly things and is not, in and of itself, a religious term.

Secularism is a belief that only worldly or natural things ex-ist. Secularism's emphasis on empirical verification leads some to conclude it is grounded in fact instead of faith. Secularists often use terms like "scientific" and "modern" concerning their points of

---

78 The movement to deny the supernatural also has other names, such as rationalism, and naturalism.

view while labeling others as "religious" and "superstitious." To the secularist, all religious beliefs are suspect.

The secularist's claim to be nonreligious comes from secularism being empirical. Since secularism restricts itself to the physical world, it rejects anything associated with the supernatural.

As we saw in the last chapter, rejecting all religious beliefs and retaining a coherent viewpoint is impossible. There are just too many beliefs that are, by their nature, religious. As such, secularism does not really reject or ignore religion, but only traditional religions. Secularism is a religious point of view and thus competes with traditional religions.

The difference is not that secularists rely on facts while others look to faith to support their positions. In some cases, one could easily make the opposite argument. Josh McDowell, a well-known Christian speaker and author, recounted the following incident in one of his books:

> At another university I was lecturing in a philosophy class. Upon my conclusion the professor immediately began to badger me with questions about the validity of the resurrection. After several minutes the discussion almost got to be obnoxious.
>
> Finally a student asked the professor what he believed took place that first Easter morning. After a brief pause, the professor honestly replied: "To tell you the truth, I really don't know." Then he immediately added rather forcefully, "But it wasn't the resurrection!"[79]

This professor's denial of the resurrection did not come from facts or evidence. He could not refute the evidence, such as that presented in chapter six, that supports the resurrection, and he could not provide, by his own admission, a rational alternative that would fit the facts. Still, he was absolutely sure that the resurrection did not occur.

---

79 Josh McDowell, *MORE Evidence that Demands a Verdict* (San Bernardino, CA: Here's Life, 1975), p. 5

The professor's assertion that there was no resurrection was a statement of faith. Since the resurrection did not fit his worldview, this professor concluded that it could not have happened.

This phenomenon is not unique to the professor or secularists. The world around us is vast and complex. To make any sense of it, we must apply some sort of structure and order. We do this naturally and often without thinking. As Burke describes this process,

> The brain imposes visual order on chaos by grouping sets of signals, rearranging them, or rejecting them. Reality is what the brain makes it... This imposition of the hypothesis on an experience is what causes optical illusions. It also modifies all forms of perception at all levels of complexity. To quote Wittgenstein once more, "You see what you want to see."[80]

Secularists frequently point out, and correctly so, that believers in God are often guilty of this. They interpret reality in a way consistent with their beliefs, and evidence that does not fit is ignored or rejected.

What they frequently ignore is that they do precisely the same thing! We all do, and it is virtually impossible to avoid. Often, secularists will argue that this is where science comes in, yet scientists, and thus science, are not immune.

> The structure represents a comprehensive view of the entire environment within which all human activity takes place. It thus directs the efforts of science in every detail. In all areas of research, from the cosmic to the sub-atomic, the structure indicates the best means of solving the puzzles which are themselves designated by the structure as being in need of solution. It provides a belief system, a guide and above all, an explanation of everything in existence. It places the unknown in an area defined by expectation and therefore more accessible to exploration.[81]

---

80   James Burke, *The Day the Universe Changed* (Boston: Little Brown and Co, 1985) p. 308
81   Burke, *Day*, p 310

This problem is, at its core, the same faced by Semmelweis, described earlier in this chapter, and Wegener mentioned in the last. It wasn't that their theories did not have the evidence to support their claims, but rather that these theories did not fit the scientific structure of their day. As such, they essentially ignored the evidence.

The point here is not that science is unreliable or that knowledge is impossible. Instead, secularism is not a different kind of thinking process. Many secularists see those who believe in god as using a distinct and inferior thinking process that they label *religious*. They see themselves as immune from such errors. Yet rather than being somehow different and unique, secularism is another competing way of understanding the reality around us.

When we get to some specific views, there are sometimes surprising parallels in the answers given by secularists and Christians. The historian Jacques Barzun has pointed out several of these "cultural continuities" between the Christian culture of the sixteenth century and our modern secular culture.

For example, some find it difficult to understand how Calvin or Luther could believe that there was no free will because God had predestined everything. Yet, is this any different from the modern view of many secularists concerning scientific determinism, which says there is no free will because the laws of nature control everything? The source is different, but the conclusion is not: There is no free will.

> Social Scientists and common folk who babble about genes or the Unconscious or "man a chemical machine" similarly account for others actions and their own as did Luther or Calvin... Modern criminology is rooted in this conviction and public opinion in the main agrees.[82]

With secularism's reliance on what they can prove by natural means, secularists can safely proclaim to know the truth. They can safely declare others to be wrong. That is until they discover they

---

82   Jacques Barzun, *From Dawn To Decadence: 500 Years of Western Cultural Life 1500 to the Present*   (New York: HarperCollins, 2000), p 30

are wrong. Once corrected, they will forget their earlier error and their fallibility. They will once again proclaim to know the truth.

In fact, when they discover such errors, this is viewed as something positive. They see such errors as examples, not of how the framework biased the outcome, but rather as examples of a self-correcting nature. An excellent example of the risks involved in relying on a worldview over the evidence is how scientists first reacted to meteorites.

The Risks of Certainty

Throughout history, people have known that sometimes rocks fall out of the sky. Most people accepted the existence of these rocks until the eighteenth century. They did not know where they came from but knew they did come.

At the beginning of the eighteenth century, scientists had a problem. They did not have a good explanation for how these rocks could have gotten into the sky so they could fall back out. Nor did they have a theory explaining how they could have always been in the sky but then fall out. In short, their view of nature did not allow for such rocks.

Therefore, the idea of rocks falling from the sky was declared impossible. As for those who had seen such rocks fall to earth, they obviously were unenlightened. As for the stones they produced, scientists simply explained them away, dismissing hard evidence of things that did not fit their theories.

Still, the confident pronouncements of scientists could not stop the meteors from falling. At the beginning of the nineteenth century, nearly two thousand meteorites landed in a single shower near L'Aigle, France.

In response to this disturbing lack of cooperation on the part of nature, they appointed a commission to investigate the matter. Finally, in light of the overwhelming evidence, the commission concluded that meteorites exist.

Scientists did not base their denial of meteorites on the evidence available at the time. Their conclusion went against the evidence. Many people have seen meteors throughout history, and many meteors were recovered.

Yet, since scientists could not explain how these rocks could have fallen from the sky, they decided they did not. They wrote off all the evidence, explained it away, or just ignored it. Faith was placed not in the evidence but in the worldview provided by the science of the time.

The worldview was more important than the evidence. Given that it was hard to show the existence of a natural phenomenon with empirical evidence, how much more challenging, if not impossible, would it be to prove the existence of the supernatural where the only evidence is experiential, philosophical, and historical?

The Supernatural

The supernatural does not fit into the secular worldview. Just like meteorites, secularists declare the supernatural does not exist. As we will see shortly, there is good evidence to support the supernatural. Still, for the secularist, the evidence for a reality other than that accessible through the five senses is written off, explained away, or ignored. Faith is placed not in the evidence but in the worldview provided by secularism.

The believer can't present any direct physical or natural evidence for the existence of the supernatural. Still, I can, along with many others, testify that the supernatural does exist because I have experienced it through prayer.

The obvious objection to this is why anyone should believe me. This would be a valid objection if I were the only person making this claim. This objection would still be valid if only a few people made such a claim.

If I were the only person to claim that rocks fell from the sky, that would not be enough evidence to accept the existence of meteorites. As the number of reports of stones falling from the sky increases, it is more reasonable to conclude that they exist.

The point here concerns the evaluation of evidence. If only one person experienced an event, then only one person could report it. On the other hand, many people experience something does not mean they understand it correctly. They could still be wrong. Generally, however, the more independent witnesses we have for an event, the more likely the event occurred as reported.

It is the same for the supernatural. As the number of reports concerning the existence of the supernatural increases, the likelihood also increases. The claims become harder to discount.

It is not just a select and limited few who have had some experience beyond the realm of the natural. Literally, billions of people from every time of human history, every part of the world, and every culture have experienced the supernatural.

The vast majority of people accept the supernatural as a part of life. If it is not the supernatural that has caused these perceptions, what has? In terms of numbers, those who doubt the existence of the supernatural makeup only a tiny minority.[83] Mostly, a person must learn to reject or ignore the supernatural.

The skeptic often replies that they see no evidence of supernatural phenomena and that those who do simply supply supernatural explanations for what are natural phenomena. Perhaps, but couldn't the reverse also be true? Could not the skeptic simply be giving natural explanations to supernatural phenomena, such as with the study on prayer and healing mentioned above? The major problem with much of this type of evidence is that it is subjective: it is subject to one's emotions and feelings.

The philosophical and historical evidence, on the other hand, is objective. This evidence does not depend on our subjective experience. Instead, it is based on our knowledge of the world and the

---

83 In one recent survey only 1% agreed with the statement that "There is no such thing as God ." George Barna, *The Barna Report 1992-93* (Ventura, CA: Regal Books, 1992) p. 273

laws of logic. Among the massive coverage of Pope John Paul II's death, news reports mentioned several interesting "coincidences."

- Just before he died in 1968, Padre Pio decided to destroy the hundreds of thousands of letters people had sent him requesting healing because they contained confidential information. Before destroying them, he selected two and told a fellow monk to hold on to them, and they would be important. The letters were from a then-unknown Polish priest, Carol Wojtyla, who later became Pope John Paul II.[84]
- According to the third secret of Fatima, there would be an assassination attempt on the Pope. Mehmet Ali Aga shot Pope John Paul II on the day of the Feast of Our Lady of Fatima.[85]
- According to a Prophecy given by St Malachy, a 12th-century Irish archbishop who is said to have had a prophecy of 112 popes, pope 110 (John Paul II) would be "de labore solis" or the labor of the sun. A solar eclipse happened on the day John Paul II was born and another on the day of his burial.[86]

Are these just coincidences, or are they signs of supernatural influence? They certainly would not be the proof that the skeptic demands.

Still, are they examples of what James Burke pointed out, "events then fit the hypothesis, or are rejected as being unrecognizable and without meaning."[87] Since things like this do not fit

---

84 http://www.hughhewitt.com/cgi-bin/calendar.
pl?month=4&view=Event&event_id=717
85 http://www.hughhewitt.com/cgi-bin/calendar.
pl?month=4&view=Event&event_id=717
86 http://www.irishcentral.com/roots/history/st-malachy-predicted-pope-benedicts-successor-will-be-last-pope-190715001-237789421
87 Burke, *Day* p. 336

the worldview of secularism, is it any wonder that secularists write them off?

The Cosmological Argument

The cosmological argument is one of the classical philosophical arguments for the existence of God. Over the years, it has taken many forms, and people have presented it in many ways. Still, the argument focuses on the reason for existence in each case.

How did we get here? Why does the universe exist? The starting point for this argument is that the universe does exist. While philosophers may debate the nature of this existence, few would seriously challenge that it does.

Any part of the universe will do for the cosmological argument, so we will use a pear for this illustration. The question we seek to answer is: How did the pear come to be here? Or, more simply, why does the pear exist? There are five possible answers to this question.

The pear could be an illusion.
The pear could be eternal.
The pear could be self-created.
The pear could be part of an infinite series of events.
The pear could be part of a finite series of events.

The first three possibilities, that the pear is either an illusion, that it is eternal, or that it was self-created, can quickly be eliminated. If the pear was simply an illusion, implying that nothing exists, the question becomes: Who or what is experiencing the illusion?

If at least the illusion exists, then we can apply the cosmological argument to the illusion itself. Where does the illusion come from? So, claiming that the pear is an illusion, while it may initially seem an answer, does not answer the question.

As for the pear creating itself, if one considers the implications of self-creation, one will quickly realize that it is not only impossible but illogical.[88] Self-creation would require that the pear affect

88 While some of the findings of quantum mechanics makes this a far more

itself before it existed! In other words, it would need an effect to be complete before there was a cause.

As for the pear being eternal, you can leave one on your counter for a few weeks to see this problem. The pear must be stable and unchanging, immune to outside forces if eternal. Since the pear changes, as scientists tell us, everything in the natural universe does; it is not eternal. When it changes, it will no longer exist in its prior form and will now be in a new form.

Thus, we conclude the pear is part of a chain of events, a series of causes and effects that have resulted in the pear. This conclusion is not that surprising. After all, the pear came from a pear tree, which grew from a seed. The seed was once in an earlier pear, which came from an earlier tree, and so on. The only question that remains is whether this chain of events is infinitely long or has a beginning.

The concept of a finite series of causes and effects is logically consistent. To see this, consider 100 dominos set up in line so that as one domino falls, it strikes the next one, which falls and hits the next, and so on. If we push the first domino, we start a finite chain of causes and effects that ends when domino number 100 falls.

If there is no outside interference, such as your cat jumping on the table where you have so carefully constructed this experiment, then before domino number 100 can fall, dominos 1 through 99 must have fallen. This sequence is both logical and what we would expect to see.

On the other hand, the concept of an infinite series of causes and effects is logically flawed. Consider our row of dominos again, except now it extends into infinity. There is no beginning, no first domino.

For a given domino in the line, let's call it domino N, we can ask the following question: Will it ever fall? Before domino N can fall, all the dominos in the sequence before it must fall. In the finite

---

complicated issue in the subatomic realm, they do not fundamentially change this argument, particularly a the level of apple.

series of 100 dominos mentioned above, dominos 1 through 99 must fall before reaching the domino.

In an endless number of dominos, an endless number of dominos must fall for an infinite sequence before reaching domino N. At first, you might think there is no problem, for there would be infinite time. Yet this comes from a misconception about infinity.

An infinite number of dominos will never finish falling, even if given an endless amount of time, that is, forever. No matter how many dominos have already fallen, there will always be an infinite number remaining to fall before reaching domino N. For domino N to fall would require the completion of an endless sequence, something which, by definition, is impossible. Something endless cannot end.

Applying this to our pear, if part of an infinite sequence of events, it would never exist since the events that must precede it would never be complete. Since it does exist, it cannot be the result of an infinite series. So our pear, and the universe, result from a finite sequence of causes and effects. As a finite series, there must have been the first cause, just as there must be the first domino in a finite number of dominos.

Historically, critics have questioned the cosmological argument on two fronts. One is to defend infinite regression, and the other is to challenge the idea that the universe had a cause. Paul Davies' book, *God & The New Physics*, is an example of the defense of infinite regression. Davies writes,

> so long as each individual member of the succession is explained then, *ipso facto*, the succession is explained. And as every member of the chain owes its existence to some preceding member or members, each member of the infinite chain *is* explained.[89]

The real problem with this type of argument is that it misses the point entirely. Davies is correct that in an infinite chain, each

89 Paul Davies, *God & The New Physics* (New York: Simon and Schuster, 1983) p.37

member is explained by reference to the member before it. Yet, the question here is whether the chain itself can be infinite or must be finite.

To put it another way, does an explanation for each member explain the overall chain? That one domino can fall and strike another does not answer whether an infinite sequence can finish. However, Davies leaves that question unanswered. How can an infinite sequence ever be completed when, by definition, an infinite sequence never ends? In short, his argument is we are here, so an infinite series must be possible, but this is hardly an answer.

Concerning the claim something caused the universe, skeptics typically question this by pointing out a supposed inconsistency in the argument. Again, as Davies points out,

> there is a logical difficulty in attributing that cause to God, for it could then be asked 'What caused God' ... the cosmological argument is founded on the assumption that everything requires a cause, yet ends in the conclusion that at least one thing (God) does not require a cause. The argument seems to be self-contradictory.[90]

The argument is only self-contradictory when phrased as "everything has a cause." We avoid Davies' objection when we restrict our discussion to the natural world requiring a cause, as in this example.

We are not looking to explain everything; we only want to explain the natural universe. Since God, as the creator of the natural universe, would not be part of the natural universe, God would not be part of the things that require a cause. There is no contradiction in the argument.

This still leaves the other part of Davies' argument, if God can exist eternally without a cause, "Why can't the universe exist without an external cause?"[91] There are two answers to this.

First and foremost is the fact that the universe has natural laws where cause and effect play a crucial role. A pear does not just fall

90   Davies, *God*, p .37
91   Davies, *God*, p .38

for no reason; it falls because of a cause. It is in a gravitational field that is pulling it down. To reject cause and effect is to deny one of the critical foundations of science.

On the other hand, one of the inherent characteristics of God is that, unlike the natural universe, God is eternal and unchanging. As such, God would not be subject to cause and effect. There is no reason to assume that what applies to the universe must also apply to God.

The second reason is similar to the first but comes more from the realm of science rather than philosophy. As detailed in the first book in this series, during the nineteenth and early twentieth centuries, scientists believed that the universe was eternal. It has always existed, as it does now.

But the evidence against an eternal universe grew, so it became untenable. Scientists now believe that the universe did have a beginning in what they call the Big Bang.

While they seek ways to avoid a beginning, the current theories still have a problem getting the whole process started in the first place, even apart from the issue of infinite regression. The recent scientific evidence is in harmony with the cosmological argument.

As we stated earlier, the cosmological argument is presented in many ways. In light of the Big Bang, a shorter way of explaining this argument is to point out that all things that have a beginning also have a cause. Since the universe had a beginning, it had a cause. This cause must be separate and distinct from the universe; otherwise, it would not have been able to cause it.

The very existence of a universe based on cause and effect shows that some entity must exist separate from the natural universe that caused or created it. While the cosmological argument does not tell us who or what this eternal creator is, it does show that an eternal creator does exist.[92]

---

92 Historically one of the problems with the cosmological argument has been that some have tried to take it too far. For example, you cannot get to

Since the First Cause must be separate from the natural universe, it cannot be part of nature. Therefore, there is something other than natural. Historically, that part of reality beyond the natural is the supernatural. If these definitions are accepted, the cosmological argument shows that the supernatural does exist.

The Cosmological argument does not reveal much about the entity that created the universe. Still, other arguments, such as the teleological argument, do. The teleological argument is an argument based on design. In short, if the natural universe shows signs of being designed, then this would indicate that there was a designer.

William Paley famously summarized this argument as a hypothetical situation in which you were to find a watch on a beach; you could justifiably conclude there was a watchmaker. The argument from design has also seen considerable support in the recent findings of science, particularly with the anthropic principle.

The anthropic principle is that when looking at the universe, it seems created to support intelligent life. Many factors in the laws of nature seem carefully tuned for life, and changing any of them by the smallest of margins would preclude life's existence.

Some explain this by claiming the universe only appears this way because we are here. If things were different, we would not be here to see it. Yet, this is hardly an explanation. Others speculate about multiple universes, where all possible universes exist. Yet, while very popular as a plot device for movies and TV, this is little more than speculation, and at least for now, not a majority view among quantum physicists.

The anthropic principle reveals a rational and intelligent creator, not just a blind mixture of natural forces combined with chance.[93]

For many, the arguments, like the cosmological or teleological arguments, are not considered seriously. They are old arguments

---

Jesus Christ, the Son of God, using only the Cosmological argument. It does demonstrate that there is more to reality than the natural world around us.

93 For more on this argument, see *Evidence for the Bible,* Consider Christianity Series, Volume 1, Chapter 4.

used long ago, but philosophers have long since refuted them. They believe then little more than historical curiosities.

Yet, like many other areas of study, philosophy is not static. As knowledge grows, philosophers are constantly modifying theories and beliefs.

In the nineteenth century, scientists rejected the particle theory of light. Then, in the early twentieth century, Einstein showed that light existed as a particle. In much the same way, new information can also change the status of philosophical theories.

The rejection of the classical arguments for the existence of God, like most things in philosophy, was strongly influenced by the intellectual environment of the time. It was a time when philosophy sought to distance itself from the religious dominance that governed the Middle Ages.

Materialism and similar views rejected the existence of anything beyond the natural world. The theories of philosophers of the time tended to limit what types of knowledge were rational, such as Kant's limiting rational knowledge to *phenomena,* information from our senses as understood by the mind. The net effect of these views was to exclude knowledge of God and the supernatural.

More recent discoveries have cast doubt on some of these theories. For example, one of the critical discoveries in Quantum physics is the uncertainty principle. The uncertainty principle `states that beyond a certain level of accuracy, we cannot know certain characteristics of sub-atomic particles.

For example, you cannot know a particle's position and velocity. Beyond a certain point, the more you know of one, the less you know of the other. If the theories limiting knowledge were correct, then the uncertainty principle should have been a stop sign for scientists, but it wasn't.

As the investigation of science progressed, some philosophers began to question many theories that formed the foundation for rejecting the classical arguments for the existence of God.

Asked about the leading contributions of philosophy in the area of religion during the latter part of the twentieth century, Dallas Willard, professor and past director of the School of Philosophy at the University of Southern California, said it was,

> no doubt the revival of serious arguments about the existence and nature of God. Twenty-five to thirty years ago, this was thought to be a completely settled issue, that there would be no rational support for the existence of God. In the last twenty-five to thirty years, people have returned to these arguments and have presented increasingly convincing interpretations of the arguments for God's existence.[94]

The reason for this change directly relates to the changes in our understanding of the universe brought about by scientists in the last century.

> Now, there are scientists who will say that it takes more faith to be an atheist than it does to be a believer. It is a combination of things, things that you might not expect, like the Big Bang theory. One interesting thing about the Big Bang theory … is that it said there was a beginning to the material universe, and it did not exist before then. Once you get that settled in your head, you begin to examine alternatives for how that came to pass.
>
> It is not just that kind of argument. All of the traditional arguments have been given convincing re-interpretations by outstanding people. That has been the single most important development.[95]

While empirical evidence for the supernatural may not be possible, it is not the only form of evidence. There is experiential, historical, and philosophical evidence for the supernatural. Accepting the supernatural is not an unreasonable or irrational position, for the evidence supports it. Is the physical world all that there is? The weight of the evidence gives a clear answer: No, there is more.

---

94   Interview with Dallas Willard, *Affirm*, May/June 1994, pp 14
95   Interview with Dallas Willard, *Affirm*, May/June 1994, pp 14-15

3

Christianity

Look to the essence of a thing, whether it be a point of doctrine, of practice, or of interpretation.
(Marcus Aurelius Antoninus A.D. 121-180)[96]

For the time will come when men will not put up with sound doctrine. *(2 Timothy 4:19)*

THE DECADE OF the seventies brought an incredible explosion of interest in the inner self. People diligently sought spiritual awareness and enlightenment. Many looked to Eastern religions such as Zen and Taoism, and others to Gurus. Some joined communes. Christianity saw a revival with the Jesus People and the Born Again movement.

With all this diversity, many people felt that it really didn't matter which movement you followed as long as you were sincere. Everyone had to seek their own path, and all paths led to God.

One of these religious movements flourished in San Francisco under the guidance of a charismatic leader named Jim. Jim preached all the right things: concern for the sick and underprivileged, help for the poor, and support for minorities. Local politicians liked him because they could count on him to bring large crowds to rallies. There was even some talk that Jim had done a few miracles.

Despite all of the popularity, a few did voice concern. Jim may have started as a Christian minister back in Indiana. Yet, somewhere along the way, he moved away from the teachings found in the book

Christians consider the inspired word of God and the foundation of their beliefs: the Bible.

A few Christians complained about his unorthodox beliefs, and some relatives complained about his total control over family members. Some of those who had attended his church talked of abuse and pressure to raise funds. Still, for the most part, these charges were ignored. Jim continued to preach love and social concerns and continued to attract followers.

All of this changed on November 18, 1978, when his followers murdered United States Congressman Leo Ryan and four others investigating reports of abuse at Jonestown, the People's Temple commune in Guyana.

When Guyanese troops arrived at Jonestown the next day, they made a gruesome discovery – the bodies of 913 people, over 200 of whom were children. Most had died from drinking cyanide-laced punch, and Jim Jones had been shot through the head by one of his inner circle.

Those who followed Jim Jones to their deaths in the jungles of Guyana may have been sincere. Still, their sincerity did not protect them from being wrong about their faith and leader.

Nor were they the only ones who may have been sincere but wrong. In the middle of the 1990s, a total of seventy-four members of The Order of the Solar Temple died in several mass suicides that ended with buildings being set on fire by remote control devices.

On March 26, 1997, Marshall Applewhite convinced thirty-eight followers to join him in getting their money together, packing their suitcases, and cleansing their bodies by drinking citrus juices. The males were castrated; everyone wore new, identical Nike sneakers and then committed suicide.

All this so they could go to a spaceship that was supposed to be hiding behind the Hale-Bopp comet.[97] These people were undoubtedly sincere enough to commit suicide for their beliefs, but sincerity is not enough.

---

97 http://en.wikipedia.org/wiki/Cult_suicide

Jim Jones may have preached about love, but he denounced the teachings of the Bible. The People's Temple was not a Christian group, even though the press often labeled it as such.

Yet, if those in the media were wrong to label the People's Temple Christian, why? What is a Christian group? Despite the importance of Christianity to the historical development of Western civilization, many people are surprisingly unaware of even its most fundamental beliefs.

You can see this in the wide variety of groups claiming to be Christian even when they deny the central teachings that have historically defined Christianity.

For Christians, the foundation for what they believe, or their doctrine, is to be found in the Bible. In the first volume of this series, we looked at whether the Bible can be trusted to provide this foundation and saw that it could. Here, we will look at some of the critical doctrines it teaches. But before we look at the individual doctrines, we need to examine the charge that defining the basic teachings of the Bible is an impossible task.

A Matter of Interpretation

Some claim that nobody knows what the Bible says. It is all just a matter of interpretation, with one interpretation being as good as another. While this belief is widespread, it is nevertheless false. It is possible to read and understand what the Bible teaches. If this is true, then why are there so many churches, each claiming to be Christian?

We should remember that the Bible describes God's dealings with his creation and covers many topics. The Bible is pretty clear on the essential teachings, such as who God is and how we can be saved. There is little dispute among Christians on these doctrines.

On other teachings, the Bible is not as clear. Sometimes, this is because we are dealing with God. As created beings, we cannot expect to entirely comprehend everything the Creator does.

At other times, it is because the doctrines are not essential to salvation and only briefly mentioned. It is on these non-essential doctrines that Christian churches differ.

The Bible is not an esoteric book teaching doctrines that only the initiated can understand. The apostle Paul stated, "we do not write you anything that you can not read or understand" (2 Corinthians 1:13).

If you accept the premise that words have a particular meaning when used in a specific context, you can understand the Bible. If you don't accept this premise, then *ALL* communication becomes impossible. The Bible was written in the everyday language of its time to convey God's truths as simply, and to as many people as possible.

One source of difficulty is that, at least for most people, the version of the Bible they read is a translation. Usually, this is not much of a problem, and the major translations all do a pretty good job of accurately translating the Bible.

Still, there are some inherent problems that translators cannot avoid entirely. For one, there is always a tension between the literal accuracy of a translation and its readability. There is also the problem that the words used to translate a passage do not entirely correspond to the original words in all their nuances.

For example, the KJV translation of the sixth commandment, "Thou shalt not kill" (Ex 20:13), is acceptable but often leads to confusion. While the Hebrew word *ratsach* (רָצַח) can be translated as kill, so can seven other Hebrew words. Of these seven words, *ratsach* is the one that would be closest to the English word murder. Thus, while the KJV translation is okay, the translation in the NIV of "You shall not murder" is better.

Some claim that because of problems such as these, everything in the Bible is simply a matter of interpretation. Usually, they justify this by challenging the meaning of every word they can. While it is true that some words can have multiple meanings, normally, this does not hinder us in communication – that is, unless someone does not want to communicate.

While a bit extreme, the following example shows the problem. If I say I'm going to run down to the store, there would be little doubt about my intentions.

Still, if this were a Biblical passage, the critic would probably question: (1) Was I going to run? (2) What I meant by down? (3) Was it really a store I was going to, or could it have been a shop? They would then use this ambiguity to ignore the passage altogether, stating that it is too vague to be clearly understood.

Another problem that often makes it seem like the Bible cannot be clearly understood is when statements are cited out of context. It is the context that gives meaning to what we say. You can make anyone say just about anything by taking them out of context.

Someone who wanted to misquote me could use the passage at the start of this section and have me say that understanding the Bible is impossible,

> nobody really knows what the Bible says. It is all just a matter of interpretation, with one interpretation being as good as another.

Clearly, this is not my position. It is the opposite of my position. Yet this sort of thing happens with the Bible all the time. While sometimes this is done deliberately, for the most part, people do this out of ignorance.

For many, the Bible is simply a collection of loosely connected statements, something akin to a smorgasbord of sayings from which they can select those that agree with what they are trying to demonstrate.

Part of this comes from the chapter and verse numbering system developed by Stephen Langton, a professor at the University of Paris, around 1227.[98] Part of this comes from the common practice

---

98 Norman Geilser and Willam Nix, *A General Introduction to the Bible*, (Chicago, Il: Moody 1986) p. 340

of teaching children to memorize verses. But for whatever reason, many see the Bible as little more than a collection of statements.

While this may be a good description of the book of Proverbs, it does not apply to the other books of the Bible. Rather than loosely connected statements, the writers gave a great deal of consideration to how they wrote. The Gospel of John, for example, was not haphazardly thrown together but has the following broad outline to its structure:

I   The Prologue: Becoming Children of God (1:11:18)

    A   The Word and becoming the Children of God

II   Revelation of Jesus (1:1910:42)

    A   Jesus is the Word – 7 Days (1:1951)
    B   Early Ministry – New replaces Old (2:14:54)
    C   Rising Opposition (5:110:42)
    D   Conclusion of Section – John the Baptist (10:4042)

III Transition – Culmination of Jesus' Public Ministry (11:112:50)

    A   Jesus' greatest miracle – The raising of Lazarus (11:154)
    B   Triumphal entry (11:5512:50)
    C   Summation of Public Ministry (12:3750)

IV   The Work of Jesus (13:120:31)

    A   The Last Supper (13:1 30)
    B   Jesus prepares His Disciples for his Departure (13:3117:26)
    C   Passion (18:120:31)

V   Epilogue: Loving God means serving others (21:125)

    A   Jesus appears to disciples by the Sea (21:114)
    B   Do you Love me? (21:1524)
    C   The greatness of Jesus (21:25)

As you can see, the Gospel has two main sections: the revelation of who Jesus is and the second his work. Between these is a short transition section. There is also a prologue that introduces the main themes and the Epilogue.

Internally, each section has its own structural features, often carefully written. John wrote the prologue as a chiasmus, balancing the various points to support a key or central point. Here is an outline of the prologue that highlights its chiastic structure.

```
1:12   Word ⇔ God
  :3       Made everything
    :45      Life ⇔ Light
      :68      John the Baptist
        :9       True light coming into the world
          :10-11 Rejected by the world and His own
            :12a    As many received him
              :12b   He gave them the right to become Children of God
            :12c    To as many as believed him
          :13      Chosen by God
        :14      Word became flesh
      :15      John the Baptist
    :16      Received grace instead of grace
  :17      Grace and truth came through Jesus
:18      God (the Word) has revealed the God.
```

Notice in this structure how the concepts leading to the central point, "He gave them the right to become the Children of God," are balanced with related concepts leading away. The section starts and ends with the Word and God. Note how the apostle mentions John the Baptist in the fourth point before the center and again in the fourth point after.

Such order and structure does not happen by chance. The central statement was not just a random thought tossed in, but its location in the prologue and this chiastic structure shows that it is a major theme in the Gospel – becoming Children of God.

Nor are such carefully constructed literary features uncommon in the Bible. Granted, it takes a lot longer to understand the context of a passage and why the author chose to write a particular passage the way they did. But when you do this, often, passages that seem vague, unclear, or confusing become suddenly clear.

Gods Many And Lords Many

As an example of how context is essential to understanding and avoiding misunderstanding what the Bible says, let us look at 1 Corinthians 8:5, where Paul writes, "as there be gods many, and lords many." (KJV) As we will see shortly, one of the critical teachings of the Bible is that there is only one God, so why would Paul write this?

Members of the *Church of Jesus Christ of Latter-Day Saints* (Mormons) and others who believe in many Gods frequently use this passage as support for their belief. Stripped from its context and standing alone like this, it certainly seems to say there are many gods. Yet, when we read the passage in context, we find that the idea that Paul was saying there are actually many gods is impossible.

1 Corinthians is a letter the Apostle Paul wrote to the church he had started in the Greek city of Corinth. The Church was having problems, and they had asked him some questions. In his reply, Paul addresses these questions. The section we now refer to as 1 Corinthians 8 was Paul's response to one of these questions and begins, "Now about food sacrificed to idols."

This was an issue for the Corinthians because, during the first century, many religions sacrificed animals to their various gods. One side effect of all these sacrifices was that they left the temples with a lot of excess meat they would sell.

Thus, the question: was it okay to eat the meat sacrificed to a false god? As Paul's argument develops, we find that while this was the main question, there was a second and more profound problem that Paul also addresses: pride.[99]

However, here, we will focus on the central part of the argument in which he mentions "many gods." Here is the critical part of Paul's argument:

---

99   Note in particular how Paul begins (1 Corinthians 8:1-4) and ends (1 Corinthians 8:9-13) his argument.

> So then, about eating food sacrificed to idols: We know that an idol is nothing at all in the world and that there is no God but one. For even if there are so-called gods, whether in heaven or on earth (as indeed there are many "gods" and many "lords"), yet for us there is but one God, the Father, from whom all things came and for whom we live; and there is but one Lord, Jesus Christ, through whom all things came and through whom we live (1 Corinthians 8:4-6).

Once put into context, we see that Paul's statement is hardly a ringing endorsement of the belief that there are many gods. Still, Mormons I have talked to try to claim some ambiguity in the passage. This ambiguity leaves them room to claim it is just a matter of interpretation and that their understanding is just as valid as any other.

However, the passage simply does not leave room for the understanding that there are many gods. Paul begins his comments about food sacrificed to idols with a powerful statement that there is only one God, "We know that an idol is nothing at all in the world and that there is no God but one."

Having established this premise, he then acknowledges what would have been evident to anyone in Corinth during the first century: there were many "so-called"[100] gods. Corinth had many temples, the most famous being the temple to Aphrodite, the goddess of love. This temple was known for its temple prostitutes. However, there were also significant temples for Asclepius, Apollo, and others.

In this context, we find Paul's statement in verse 5, "For even if there are so-called gods, whether in heaven or on earth (as indeed there are many 'gods' and many 'lords')."

The structure here is: For even if A, as there are B. In such a structure, B refers to A, where A is the theoretical, and B is the actual. As such, the latter part's 'many gods and many lords' can only refer to the things called gods in the previous part of the statement.

---

100 Greek word is legomenoi - λεγόμενοι.

He is talking about food sacrificed to idols and is acknowl-
edging the obvious: people called these idols gods. As if this were
not clear enough, Paul then makes yet another statement of the
Christian belief of monotheism, "yet for us, there is but one God."

So, when put into context, the passage is not vague at all.
Clearly, Paul is referring to the gods to whom the meat in question
was sacrificed, and his point is that these are false gods and do not
exist; they are "nothing at all in the world."

It does not matter whether or not the meat was sacrificed to
something that does not exist; therefore, it is ok to eat it. Paul's
argument can be broken down as follows:

> There is only one God.
> Our God is the true God (implied premise)
> Therefore, all other gods are nothing.
>
> If the other gods are nothing, then the meat is not defiled.
> If the meat is not defiled, then it is OK to eat.

Trying to claim that Paul said there are many gods misses
the context and destroys his argument. His argument depends on
these other gods being nothing. If the other gods exist, then Paul's
reasoning that the meat is ok to eat falls apart.

So whether one is looking at the statements in context or the
argument's reasoning, it is not "just a matter of interpretation"
whether or not Paul supports the belief that many gods exist.

Again, I am not claiming that every passage in the Bible is as
clear as this one. Sometimes, we do not know enough about the
historical context to understand precisely what is said. Sometimes,
we do not know exactly how to translate a passage. In these cases,
there is room for legitimate disagreement.

Since the areas of disagreement tend to get much more discussion than the areas of agreement, this leads to the perception that
everything is simply a matter of interpretation. But it is fallacious
to conclude that because some passages are ambiguous, they all are.

Not everything is subject to interpretation, and in a great many areas, the Bible is clear.

A significant problem that leads to confusion concerns one's initial approach to the Bible. While common today, the main question when trying to understand the Bible should not be: What does it mean to me? It makes little difference what I think or what you think a passage should say. The real question that matters is: What was the author trying to say? When there is a dispute over what a particular passage says, read it for yourself, in context, seeking the author's intent. Often, this will settle the issue.

For those times when a statement is still unclear, biblical scholars use rules to try to understand them. Most of these rules are simply common sense. For example, if there are two statements on a subject, one is pretty clear in what it says, while the other is somewhat vague, you interpret the vague statements in light of the clear one. Another rule is never to base a doctrine on a single passage, especially a vague one, and then interpret the rest of the Bible to fit it.

When these simple rules of interpretation are employed, the teachings of the Bible are clear, at least for the central doctrines we will look at shortly. There is very little dispute on these central beliefs.

These doctrines have defined Christianity as a religion. Groups that accept these doctrines are considered Christian groups. Those who do not accept these doctrines cannot be considered Christians, at least not in any historical sense.

Some may consider it judgmental and arrogant to say who is or is not a Christian simply because they do not accept a particular doctrine or belief.

First, let it be clear this concerns classifying groups based on beliefs. After all, if there is a difference between being a Christian, Jew, Muslim, Buddhist, or Hindu, does it not mean that Christians must have some distinct beliefs in contrast with these other religions?

Second, we are not talking about an individual's relationship with God. This is a spiritual matter that only God can judge, for only He knows what is truly in a person's heart. We may get a good indication from a person's actions or beliefs, but we cannot judge the heart.

Groups do not have personal relationships with God, and what defines a religious group are the group's beliefs. If we were utterly non-judgmental, we would conclude any group claiming to be Christian was, regardless of what they believed.

This attitude would render the term "Christian" completely meaningless, for something that can mean anything means nothing. Should we consider a group that believed in child sacrifice to be Christian? Would this make child sacrifice a legitimate expression of the teachings of Christ on par with caring for the poor? Certainly not.

So the question is not should a line be drawn defining Christianity, but where do we draw that line? If we draw no line, Christianity becomes a meaningless term that could be applied to any group or action, from the most divine to the most depraved.

On the other hand, if we compose a long and extensive list of doctrines that one must accept to be considered Christian, we would indeed be arrogant and judgmental. We would restrict Christianity to groups that agreed with us in every detail. The doctrines that define Christianity should be limited to those expressed in the Bible as essential.

Essential Teachings

Basically, four beliefs have defined Christianity as a religion for nearly 2,000 years. All the other teachings and beliefs of Christianity come from these four beliefs. They are briefly summarized as follows:

❖　　　The doctrine of the Trinity best represents the nature of God: that there is only one God, but within the one

God exists three persons: the Father, the Son, and the Holy
Spirit.

❧   Jesus Christ is the only Son of God, who died on
the cross for our sins and rose again bodily in victory over
death.

❧   Man is a sinner in need of salvation, and salvation
is only made possible by the death of Jesus. We can obtain
salvation only by grace through faith.

❧   The Bible is the inspired word of God.

Most people have heard of these doctrines at one time or another. Still, though these teachings have been around for nearly
two thousand years, there has been much confusion.

Much of this confusion comes from semi-Christian religions[101]
that describe their beliefs using the same terminology as Christians. While they may use the same words, they have changed their
meanings to something completely different from what Christians
have historically believed.

I have talked to many Mormons who would agree with many of
the four statements above.[102] Yet the teachings of Latter Day Saints
on each of these doctrines vastly differ from what Christianity has
historically taught.[103]

These Mormons were not trying to be deceptive; instead, their
church has redefined these terms. For example, when a Latter Day
Saint uses the phrase "Son of God" as defined by their church,[104]

---

101 The term semi-Christian religion is used here in a technical sense and
is not intended to be a prejudicial term. The term simply refers to a group
which, although they claim to be Christian, rejects some or all of the doctrines
and teachings which have historically defined Christianity as a religion.

102 Most Mormons would probably agree with points 2 - 4.

103 There are many good books on differences between the Latter Days Saints
doctrine and Christian doctrine. Two good books are: Martin, Walter, *The
Kingdom of the Cults* (Minneapolis: Bethany Fellowship, 1977) and Tanner,
Jerald and Sandra, *The Changing World of Mormonism* (Chicago: Moody Press,
1980)

104 Mormon doctrine teaches that Jesus is literally a son of God the Father
and Mother, created out of their union. Since Mormon doctrine also teaches
that we were created out of this union, Jesus is literally our spirit brother. For

they mean something completely different than the historic Christian definition of this phrase. Because of this, a Mormon and a Christian can believe Jesus is the Son of God and still disagree on who Jesus is.

So that there is no confusion as to what the basic teachings of Christianity are, let us take a closer look at each of these doctrines. This overview will not, by any means, be an exhaustive survey.[105] Hopefully, it will be enough to clarify these doctrines and demonstrate why Christians believe them.

The Trinity

One of the foundational beliefs of any religion is its belief about God. Christianity declares that God exists, created the universe, and continues to interact with His creation today.

Through revelation, God has shown Himself to exist as what has historically come to be called the Trinity. The Doctrine of the Trinity teaches that there is only one God. Within the nature of the one God, three distinct, separate, and equal persons exist: the Father, the Son, and the Holy Spirit.

While no single statement in the Bible states, "God exists as the Trinity," the doctrine is clearly taught. The Trinity is the only explanation that considers all of the Bible's teachings concerning God.

Put simply, the Bible states that there are three separate and equal persons: the Father, the Son, and the Holy Spirit. Each of these persons is God, yet there is only one God. What explanation would fit other than the doctrine of the Trinity?

---

the historical Christian teaching see the section on Jesus Christ, later in this chapter.
105 There are many excellent books out on the doctrines of Christianity. A very good place to start would be: Walter Martin, *Essential Christianity* (Santa Ana, CA: Vision House, 1980) For those who wish a more in depth study: J. Oliver Buswell, *A Systematic Theology of the Christian Religion.* (Grand Rapids, MI: Zondervan, 1962) or Millard J. Erickson, Christian Theology (Grand Rapids, MI: Baker, 1985)

Few would disagree that the Father, the Son, and the Holy Spirit are three separate persons.[106] Matthew demonstrates this in his description of the baptism of Jesus. Just after John the Baptist baptized Jesus in the river Jordan, the Father spoke from heaven, saying, "This is my Son, whom I love; with him I am well pleased." At the same time, the Holy Spirit descended on Jesus "like a dove" (Matthew 3:16-17).

We can see in this account that Matthew mentions all three persons of the Trinity in different locations simultaneously. This account demonstrates that they are three separate persons.

When Jesus stated that His will was in subjection to the will of His Father (Luke 22:42), He demonstrated the existence of two separate wills and, therefore, two separate persons. In John 8:17-18 Jesus said that he and his Father were two witnesses. Also, unless you believe that Jesus was praying to himself, the prayers of Jesus to the Father (John 17) demonstrate that Jesus and the Father are different persons.

That the Father is God is clearly and directly stated in, for example, Peter's use of the phrase "God the Father" (2 Peter 1:17). The deity of Jesus Christ is also an inescapable teaching of the Bible. John opens his gospel with his description of the Word, "In the beginning was the Word, and the Word was with God, and the Word was God" (John 1:1). John goes on to identify the Word as Jesus Christ (John 1:14-15, 30-31).

Jesus is not only God; He is the God of the Hebrew Scriptures.[107] When on Mount Sinai, Moses asked God His name so he could say who sent him to free the Israelites. God answered, "*I AM WHO I AM*," and told Moses to say that "*I AM*" had sent him (Exodus 3:14).

---

106 Some, like the United Pentecostal Church do dispute the existence of three Persons, and instead claim that Jesus sometimes appears in the role of the Father or in the role of the Holy Spirit. Because of this, and other reasons, they were expelled from the Assembly of God in the early part of this century.
107 For examples of the Trinity in the Old Testament see Genesis 1 and Proverbs 30:1-4.

In the book of Isaiah, especially chapters 40-55, God refers to himself as "I am he." See, for example, Isaiah 43:10. When these passages were later translated into Greek, the language of the New Testament, they were translated as the Greek words *ego eimi* (ἐγὼ εἰμί), which means "I am."

One day in the temple, Jesus disputed with the Jewish leaders. They pointed out that they were children of Abraham and asked him, "Who do you think you are?" Jesus told them, "I tell you the truth, before Abraham was born, I AM" (John 8:53-58).

Here, Jesus referred to himself as *ego eimi* (I AM), precisely the Greek words used by God in the Greek translation of Isaiah. At that point, the Jewish leaders picked up stones to kill Jesus. There are only two choices: either they wanted to stone Jesus for improper grammar, I AM instead of I WAS, or because he claimed to be I AM, the God who had appeared to Moses and Isaiah.

During another dispute in the temple, the Jewish leaders once again picked up stones in an attempt to kill Jesus. But Jesus stopped them, asking, "I have shown you many great miracles from the Father. For which of these do you stone me?" The Jews replied that they were not stoning him for any of the works he had performed. They were stoning him, "because you, a mere man, claim to be God" (John 10:31-33). Clearly, the Jews understood the claims that Jesus made about himself.

At least eight passages in the New Testament directly state the deity of Jesus Christ.[108] Paul wrote to Titus, a disciple he had left on the island of Crete to organize a church, "We wait for the blessed hope – the glorious appearing of our great God and Savior, Jesus Christ" (Titus 2:13). In the book of Hebrews, God the Father says of His Son "Your throne, O God, will last forever and ever" (Hebrews 1:8). The Bible teaches that Jesus is God the Son.

Although the Bible does not express the deity of the Holy Spirit as often as the deity of Jesus Christ, it is still clearly set forth. In

---

108 John 1:1, John 1:18, John 20:28, Romans 9:5, Titus 2:13, 2 Peter 1:1, Hebrews 1:8, 1 John 5:20.

the book of Acts, Luke describes the situation in the early Church. In one instance, two converts, Ananias and Sapphira, attempted to deceive the church. Peter confronted them, saying, "You have lied to the Holy Spirit... You have not lied to men but to God" (Acts 5:1-4).

The Bible teaches three persons, the Father, the Son, and the Holy Spirit, are God. Typically, this would lead us to conclude that the Bible teaches polytheism, the belief in many gods. The Mormons have concluded this, for they believe three gods exist.[109] The Bible, however, teaches that there is only one God.

That the Hebrew Scriptures teach there is only one God can hardly be questioned. One of the distinguishing features of the Jewish religion is its strict monotheism.

This strict monotheism is carried into the New Testament as well. Jesus referred to the "praise that comes from the only God" (John 5:44). As we have already seen, Paul stated, "We know that an idol is nothing at all in the world and that there is no God but one" (1 Corinthians 8:4). James said of the belief in one God that "Even the demons believe that – and shudder" (James 2:19).

The main problem with the Trinity is that it is understandably difficult to comprehend because it is beyond our realm of experience. Because of this, people use many analogies to help understand the Trinity.

One analogy I often use is that of lines in different dimensions. In a one-dimensional universe, only length would exist. The only types of objects that could exist (besides a single point) would be lines.

There would be no such thing as a two-lined object because, as seen in Figure 3.1, when we join two lines, they become a single, long line. In a one-dimensional universe, the number of lines equals the number of objects.

---

109 The Latter Day Saint doctrine could also be classified as henotheism, the belief in many gods with the worship of one, for they see the Father, Son, and Holy Spirit as a single "Godhead." Mormon doctrine teaches there are many gods and Mormon males will, if they follow the teaching of the church, become gods themselves, but they worship only one "Godhead."

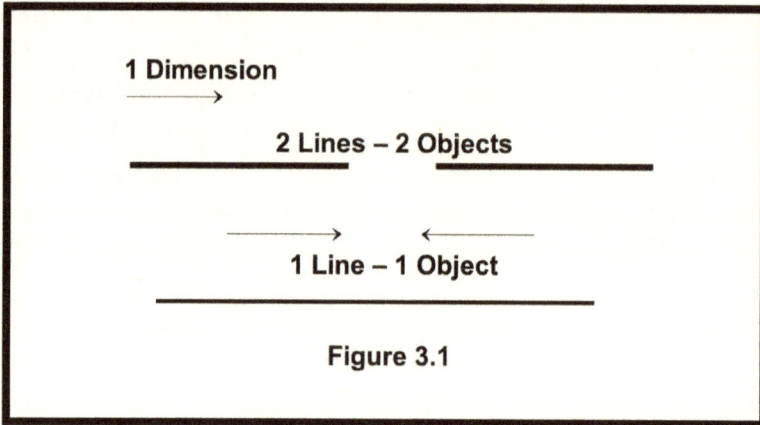

1 Dimension

2 Lines – 2 Objects

1 Line – 1 Object

Figure 3.1

If we add a second dimension, width, we can now join lines at angles to make objects other than just lines. For example, we could join three lines end to end to create a triangle, as seen in Figure 3.2.

A triangle is a single object made up of three distinct lines. From a one-dimensional point of view, this makes no sense. Three lines can't be in a single object and remain separate lines. From a two-dimensional point of view, three different lines and one object are no problem at all.

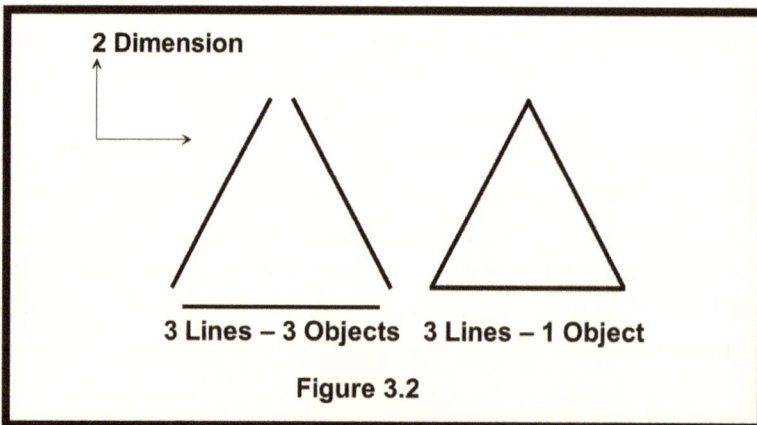

2 Dimension

3 Lines – 3 Objects   3 Lines – 1 Object

Figure 3.2

When we apply this concept to our understanding of the Trinity, we see the concept of three separate persons existing as a single

God is not impossible. God is not limited to our 3-dimensional world, so there is no reason to see this as improbable.

It is essential to point out here that this is only an analogy, and as with all analogies, it breaks down if pressed too far. In this case, while you have three lines and one object, the individual lines are only part of the object. Individual lines are just that, individual lines. Only together are they a triangle. Yet the three persons of the Trinity are not parts of God; they are God.

Fundamentally, this conception of God is beyond our understanding because it is a conception of God beyond our experience. Analogies can help to some extent, but they remain just analogies. That we cannot understand something, particularly something fundamental, does not make it wrong.

Much of Quantum Mechanics does not make sense and sometimes seems contradictory. In the nineteenth century, the central scientific question was whether light was a particle, like a grain of sand, or a wave, a force moving through a media, as a wave moves through water. In short, does it act at a point, like a bullet, or along a line like a shock wave?

By the end of the century, scientists had conclusively shown light acted as a wave, eliminating the particle theory. Then Einstein showed light can act as a particle. Somehow, it is both. How can that be? It does not make sense. We may not understand it, but that is what it is.

The situation with the Trinity is similar. We may not understand this concept of God, yet that is what the Bible teaches. Thus, if you think you know the Trinity, that is a good indication that there is a problem.

Some people have told me that the doctrine of the Trinity only proves that the Bible contradicts itself. To them, the doctrine of the Trinity is simply the result of theologians trying to reconcile those contradictions. In the process, they have come up with something completely incomprehensible.

This argument might have some validity if one writer claimed that both the Father and Jesus were God, while a different writer claimed there is only one God. But this is not what we find. The Trinity is supported throughout much of the New Testament and, to some extent, even the Hebrew Scriptures.[110] It would be no problem to restrict ourselves to a single author, like Paul or John, and still demonstrate the doctrine of the Trinity.

Rather than demonstrating how the Bible contradicts itself, the doctrine of the Trinity demonstrates the harmony of the authors. Even for such a complex and challenging teaching, the different authors agree entirely.

Throughout history, the doctrine of the Trinity has been one of the most controversial of the basic teachings of Christianity. This controversy is due mainly to the fact that the Trinity is beyond our ability to comprehend fully. We can know that there are three persons and yet only one God, but we cannot understand it. As the noted author, C. S. Lewis stated, this was,

> one of the reasons I believe Christianity. It is a religion you could not have guessed. If it offered us just the kind of universe we had always expected, I should feel we were making it up.[111]

The fact that we cannot understand the nature of God should not be too troubling, for the creation should not expect to understand the creator. When we find that the Christian doctrine of the Trinity is beyond our comprehension, this should be evidence for the veracity of Christianity, as it was for C. S. Lewis.

As in so many instances, this is a Catch-22 situation. Many critics claim that since the Trinity is beyond our comprehension, it does not make sense and must be false. Yet, if the Christian concept of God were a nice neat package, one we could easily understand, it

---

110 For examples of the Trinity in the Old Testament see Genesis 1 and Proverbs 30:1-4.

111 C S Lewis, *Mere Christianity* (New York, New York: Macmillan, 1952) pp. 47-8

would be cited as proof that people had created God in their own image, and again, it must be false. Either way, critics will criticize Christianity.

One remaining issue is that some have objected to including the Trinity in this list. There is at least the possibility of a valid objection in that, as mentioned above, the word Trinity does not appear in the Bible. Still, the beliefs that make up the doctrine of the Trinity, that three separate and equal persons exist: the Father, the Son, and the Holy Spirit. Each of these persons is God, yet there is only one God, are taught in the Bible.

The vast majority of Christians believe in the Trinity. Whether one wants to use the term Trinity or something else is irrelevant. The question remains: what do you think about God? Does this belief conflict with what the Bible teaches?

Jesus Christ

Central to the beliefs of Christianity is the nature and role of Jesus Christ. As we have seen, Christianity teaches that Jesus Christ is God the Son, who took the form of a man and lived among His creation (John 1:1-3 and John 1:14, Philippians 2:6-8).

The story of His life, death, and resurrection are well known, and we need not go into great detail here. What often is not appreciated is the importance of these events to the Christian faith.

I have talked to many people who believe that Jesus was a good man or that the world would be better if more people followed His moral teachings. But the heart of the Christian faith is not the moral teachings of Jesus. While important, they are only secondary.

If Jesus had been primarily a moral teacher, this would not have required Him to be God. There would have been no need for the virgin birth, and the miracles He did would have served little purpose. Finally, His death would only have been a tragic end to a promising ministry.

Paul tells us that the death of Jesus was not a tragic end. Instead, it was a central part of Christ's purpose on earth. Paul writes:

> For what I received I passed on to you as of *first importance*:
> that Christ died for our sins according to the Scriptures, that
> he was buried, that he rose again on the third day according to
> the Scriptures. (1 Corinthians 15:3-4 Italics added)

Christianity is not simply a nice set of moral teachings. Christianity teaches that man is a sinner in need of salvation. Christ came to provide the means for that salvation through His death on the cross. That Jesus is God is essential because only God can bear the punishment for all sins. The virgin birth was necessary as the means by which God entered the world. The miracles testified that Jesus is the Messiah.

As we saw earlier, Jesus claimed to be the God who had appeared to Moses in the Hebrew Scriptures. If He is not God, then as C. S. Lewis pointed out,

> He would either be a lunatic – on a level with the man
> who says he is a poached egg – or else he would be the Devil
> of Hell. You must make your choice. Either this man was,
> and is the Son of God: or else a madman or something worse.
> You can shut Him up for a fool, you can spit at Him and kill
> Him as a demon; or you can fall at His feet and call Him Lord
> and God. But let us not come with any patronizing nonsense
> about His being a great human teacher. He has not left that
> open to us. He did not intend to.[112]

As Paul stated in his letter to the church in the Greek city of Corinth, the heart of Christianity is not the moral teachings of Jesus but his victory over death in the resurrection (1 Corinthians 15:3-4). Greek philosophy of the time taught that only the soul was immortal, not the body.

Because of this, some in the church at Corinth thought they could discard the resurrection as unnecessary. In his response, Paul wrote,

> if Christ has not been raised, our preaching is useless and
> so is your faith… And if Christ has not been raised, your faith

112 Lewis, *Mere,* p. 56

is futile; you are still in your sins. Then those also who have
fallen asleep in Christ are lost. If only for this life we have
hope in Christ, we are to be pitied more than all men (1 Corinthians 15:14, 17-19).

The Bible teaches that not only is Jesus God the Son, but that
He became a man and lived among His creation, and he died on
the cross for the world's sins and rose from the dead three days later.
This is the Jesus of the Bible.

Salvation

Christ died for our sins, but how do we take advantage of
that? How can we know that we will go to heaven? Many hope
they are good enough to go to heaven, or at least not bad enough
to go to hell.

But the Bible does not teach us just to hope; we should know.
The apostle John wrote: "I write these things to you who believe in
the name of the Son of God so that you may know that you have
eternal life" (1 John 5:13).

How can anyone know if they are good enough? How could
anyone be assured they are good enough to go to heaven? The simple
answer is that they can't. Based on the statements of the Bible, the
only assurance we can have is that when judged, we will not pass
the test. Instead, we will all fail miserably.

Paul wrote in his letter to the church in Rome, "There is no
difference, for all have sinned and fall short of the glory of God"
(Romans 3:23) and "Therefore no one will be declared righteous in
his sight by observing the law; rather through the law we become
conscious of sin" (Romans 3:20). Anyone who has ever committed
even a single sin will not meet God's perfect standard.

But what is sin? Sin as a concept has fallen in popularity and
is currently out of fashion. People rarely use the concept of evil to
explain people's actions. When someone goes on a killing spree,
savagely butchering innocent bystanders, there will be many explanations for why they may have done it.

These explanations will include almost every possible reason except for one: that the killer was an evil person. As a society, we have, to a large extent, lost the ability to pass moral judgments. Good and evil no longer exist; only good and not-so-good exist today.

Christianity not only accepts the existence of evil but teaches that humans are, from God's point of view, basically corrupted. This view does not mean that people cannot be good, for this is a teaching about underlying inclinations.

We must teach people to be good; it is a lesson no one learns perfectly. Anyone who has raised children knows they are naturally rebellious. Parents do not have to teach a child to get into trouble.[113] Instead, they must exert considerable effort, teaching them to avoid it.

It is the rebellious nature that God considers evil, and the acts of rebellion against God, the breaking of the laws He has set forth, that He considers sin. The apostle John wrote to the early church, "Everyone who sins breaks the law; in fact, sin is lawlessness" (1 John 3:4).

The Christian concept of sin does not just include actions that one does. James was the brother[114] of Jesus and the leader of the early church in Jerusalem. Writing to early Jewish converts, he pointed out that "anyone, then, who knows the good he ought to do and doesn't do it, sins" (James 4:17).

Here, we come to an obvious question. If no one is good enough, then how can anyone be saved? Simply put, salvation is not based on what we have done or will do; salvation depends on what Christ did for us. "For God so loved the world that he gave his one and only Son, that whoever believes in him shall not perish but have eternal life" (John 3:16).

---

113 This is not to say that one cannot teach a child evil. Racism, for example, can be taught to a child.

114 The Greek word translated brother, could also refer to a close relative such as a cousin.

Salvation comes not by being good and obeying all the rules but by accepting the sacrifice Jesus made on our behalf. As Paul wrote, "For it is by grace you have been saved, through faith—and this not from yourselves, it is the gift of God—not by works, so that no one can boast" (Ephesians 2:8-9).

Many have tried to add something to this simple means of salvation throughout history. Many people find this just too easy to be acceptable. One of the first things that semi-Christian religions, and even some Christian groups, do is add all kinds of conditions for salvation.

You must get baptized, or you must take communion regularly, or you must obey this or that set of rules. This problem is not new and had already begun appearing in the early Church.

A clear example of the addition of requirements for salvation occurred in the early churches of Galatia, now central Turkey. Some in these churches required adherence to Jewish law. In response, Paul wrote his letter to the Galatians. He forcefully states that salvation is by faith in Jesus Christ alone. (see Galatians 2:16; 2:21; 3:10-11)

The Bible

The last major doctrine we will examine concerns the Bible. In the first volume of this series, we examined the claims for the reliability of the Bible in more detail. Here, we will look at the vital role that the Bible has played in Christianity. Christianity is a "book religion." We saw with the first three doctrines that the Bible is central to any teaching.[115]

The Bible is the standard that defines Christianity. For Christians, when someone claims to speak for God, whether or not they believe them should not depend on how good they sound but on whether or not what they say agrees with the word of God as recorded in the Bible.

---

115 Catholicism adds to this the teaching of the Pope, and Church tradition, but the Bible still plays a central role.

That many will try to claim divine authority is to be expected, and was even predicted by the apostle Paul long ago when he wrote,

> For the time will come when men will not put up with sound doctrine. Instead, to suit their own desires, they will gather around them a great number of teachers to say what their itching ears want to hear. They will turn their ears away from the truth and turn aside to myths. (2 Timothy 4:3-4)

A popular misconception is that Christians must stop thinking and accept unquestioningly everything handed down from the pulpit. This is not what the Bible teaches; instead, the Bible teaches the exact opposite.

We are not to accept everything but rather to "Test everything and hold on to the good" (1 Thessalonians 5:21). Luke tells us that the Christians in the Greek city of Berea were "of more noble character" than those who lived in Thessalonica. This was because the Christians at Berea "received the message with great eagerness and examined the Scriptures every day to see if what Paul said was true" (Acts 17:11).

Christians are to test, but they are to test using a fixed standard. That standard is the Bible. All teachings of the Christian faith must conform to the teachings of the Bible. Many consider this dependence on the Bible, or any book, in and of itself, irrational.

Yet, it is only irrational if you consider the Bible "just a book." From the perspective of a secularist, the Bible is just another book written by men. The secularist can see no rational reason why the Bible should hold any unique position above any other book.

One response to this argument is to point out that at least Christians have a foundation for their beliefs. While secularists may reject the foundation Christians use, what do they point to as an alternative?[116]

Still, the main problem is that for Christians, the Bible is not just another book written by men but a book that God inspired. In his letter to the church in Rome, Paul wrote that the books of

116 We will expand more on this question in Chapter Seven

the Old Testament were not the theories of men concerning God but were "the very word of God" (Romans 3:2).

The early Christians also saw the New Testament as inspired by God and, thus, Scripture. Peter, in his letter to the Christians in Asia Minor, stated concerning the writings of Paul:

> Paul also wrote you with the wisdom that God gave him. He writes the same way in all his letters, speaking in them of these matters. His letters contain some things that are hard to understand, which ignorant and unstable people distort, as they do the other Scripture. (2 Peter 3:17)

Peter saw the writings of Paul as Scripture and thus had the same status as the Hebrew Scriptures. Paul clearly described the role of the Bible in the life of a Christian in his letter to Timothy:

> All Scripture is God-breathed and useful for teaching, re-buking, correcting, and training in righteousness, so the man of God may be thoroughly equipped for every good work. (2 Timothy 3:16)

The Bible is essential to Christians because they see it as the word of God. As the word of God, they trust the Bible as a source of God's instructions to the Church and believers. The real complaint of the critic should not be that Christians place such great faith in a book but that they place their faith in God.

If the Bible is indeed the inspired word of God, not only would it be reasonable to place one's faith in it, but not to do so would be foolish. Only the most arrogant and ardent rationalist could find fault with someone who would rather trust God's judgment than their own. Thus, what is truly at issue is not the Bible's importance but whether it is God's word.

Conclusion

The four areas of belief we have examined form the core be-liefs that have defined Christianity as a religion for 2000 years. Christian denominations such as the Catholics, Anglicans, Episcopalians, Greek Orthodox, Lutheran, Methodist, Presbyterian, Baptist, Congregationalist, Assembly of God, and all others accept these four doctrines.[117]

Philip Schaff surveyed various Christian churches' doctrinal statements and creeds through the ages in his three-volume work, *Creeds of Christendom*. He refers to their ecumenical creeds as those containing "the fundamental articles of the Christian faith, as necessary and sufficient for salvation."[118] As to the acceptance of these creeds, Schaff points out that they,

> are to this day either formally or tacitly acknowledged in the Greek, the Latin, and the Evangelical Protestant Churches, and form a bond of union between them.[119]

The differences that divide denominations are mostly peripheral issues, such as when you should get baptized or whether Christians should use some spiritual gifts today. The Church is unified over the core teachings. As such, the arguments presented here and in this series do not apply to a single denomination but to Christianity in general.

---

117 As I am not a theologian and have not made an in-depth study of each of these denominations, there may be minor aspects of the presentation above with which some denominations might find fault. Also some leaders of these denominations may not accept these doctrines. The denominations themselves, in their doctrinal statements, all affirm the essence of these doctrines.
118 Philip Schaff, *Creeds of Christendom* (New York: Harper & Brothers, 1877) pp. 12-13
119 Schaff, *Creeds*, pp. 12-13

4

The Church

I call Christianity the one great curse, the one enormous and innermost perversion, the one great instinct of revenge, for which no means are too venomous, too underhand, too underground and too petty — I call it the one immortal blemish of mankind.
(Friedrich Nietzsche)[120]

THE EARLY 1800S were a time of great religious ferment in America. As the last of the states dropped their official religions, various new religious movements arose. The Shakers came to New England hoping to find Utopia and prospered for a time.

The preacher and socialist John Noyes sought his utopia in the small New York town of Oneida. While his idea of "complex marriage" did not last, the silverware company his followers started did all right.

Methodist circuit preachers rode from town to town, preaching the Gospel and baptizing. They held revival meetings wherever they could get a group of people together.

One circuit preacher, Peter Cartwright, claimed in his autobiography to have preached over 14,000 sermons and baptized over 12,000 people during his ministry. Cartwright preached throughout Kentucky and Illinois, serving several terms in the general assembly. In a life marked by victory, he suffered only one major defeat. In 1846, he ran for Congress but lost to Abraham Lincoln.

---

120 Friedrich Nietzsche, *The Antichrist: A Curse on Christianity,* 1895

In 1820, all this excitement over religion reached the small town of Manchester in Western New York State. There, a young boy named Joseph was becoming curious about religion. As the preachers in the different churches competed for members, interest in religion grew in the community.

This competition only increased Joseph's confusion. Which church should he join? Baptist? Methodist? Presbyterian? What if he chose the wrong church? As he was to record later in his life,

> In the midst of this war of words and tumult of opinions, I often said to myself: What is to be done? Who of all these parties are right, or are they all wrong together? If any of them be right, which is it, and how shall I know it?[121]

In the end, Joseph Smith concluded that all the churches were wrong, and ten years later, he founded the *Church of Jesus Christ of Latter-Day Saints* (Mormons), which he declared to be the true church of God.

The confusion experienced by Joseph Smith over the true church, which one was God's, was mainly based on a misunderstanding of the New Testament concept of the church.

A Church or The Church

In the New Testament there are two types of churches: the universal and the local. While these two overlap, they are not identical.

The universal church consists of the entire body of believers. Anyone who has accepted Jesus Christ as their personal Lord and Savior is automatically a part of the universal church.[122] When the Bible speaks of the church in a general sense, it refers to the universal church. The universal church has no physical existence apart from the believers themselves. There are no buildings for the universal church.

The local church, on the other hand, is simply a group of professing Christians who have organized and meet regularly to

---

121 Quoted in William Berrett, *The Restored Church* (Deseret Press, 1961) p. 8
122 See Acts 9:31 and 1 Corinthians 10:32

worship. When Paul wrote to the church in the city of Corinth, he wrote to a local church.

The New Testament says little about the structure and organization of the local church or about how to conduct services. These are matters largely left up to the local church to do as it sees fit. Even the day of worship is not specified. Although most early churches worshipped on Sunday, and most churches still follow this tradition today, it is neither mandatory nor universal.

The apostle Paul noted this when he wrote that the day of the week you worship is not essential. What is important is *that* you worship, and "each one should be fully convinced in his own mind... Therefore stop passing judgment on one another" (Romans 14:5&13).

What we today refer to as denominations are not different universal churches; they are various types of local churches. Denominations should not compete over which one is the "true" church. They coexist, offering different ways and styles of worship.

Someone who prefers a highly structured, ritual-oriented worship might be happy in a Catholic or Episcopal Church. Another person might find this type of service much too stuffy. As in many Baptist churches, they might prefer a service that stresses the Bible's teaching.

On the other hand, someone else might want a service that involves them both intellectually and emotionally. They might prefer the style of worship found in a charismatic church, such as the Assemblies of God.

This is not to say that the different denominations do not have doctrinal differences; they do. Thus, there is more than one consideration when looking for a church, as in many things. Still, the issues that divide these local churches are, for the most part, peripheral.

One of the significant divisions among modern denominations, though it has died down considerably, is whether Christians should speak in tongues or if tongues were only for the early church.

Unfortunately, Christians have split and formed new churches for some of the most trivial reasons. There is even one often repeated instance, though possibly mythical, of a church that split over whether Adam had a belly button! Still, even with all this division, Christians agree on the essential doctrines.

When choosing a church, the question is not as Joseph Smith described it, which is the true church. As long as the church you choose teaches the essential doctrines taught in the Bible,[123] it is a matter of in which church it is easier to worship. A church whose style of worship is right for one person may not be so for someone else.

Local churches are reflections of the universal church. Putting all the local churches together would give you the universal church in an ideal world, but this world is not ideal. As a result, the lines between the local and universal churches are blurry.

Some are believers and part of the universal church, yet do not belong to or attend any local church. Likewise, there are those who, although they may attend a local church, are not believers and, therefore, are not members of the universal church.

Since the Bible says little about the organization and structure of local churches, these organizations are mainly human creations. As human creations, church institutions are not immune from the problems of sin. It is unsurprising that throughout history, all the same issues of corruption and abuse of power that have faced all other institutions involving people also plagued the church.

The Church in the World

Even with the problems of sin, the local church is not the corrupt and worthless institution, some claim. A vast amount of good has been and continues to be done by Christians working through their local churches.

Each day, millions of people around the world are fed and cared for by people and organizations supported by and through

---

123 See Chapter Three

local churches. Local churches minister to the poor, sick, homeless, hungry, alcoholics, drug addicts, convicts in prison, and abused women and children.

In fact, for just about any social need, some part of the local church is trying to reach out to meet that need. The local church tries to do what it can to help ease people's suffering and meet their needs, the most important of which is the need for salvation through Jesus Christ.

For the rest of this chapter, I will refer only to local churches and use the word church to refer to the local church. Some people see the church as an oppressive structure suppressing true Christianity. It has used its power to extract money.

This is not true. Concerning money, the truth is the vast majority of pastors and missionaries make, according to a national survey, "far below the averages for most other professionals and below many craftsmen and laborers."[124]

To be sure, a few make a lot of money, but they are the rare, albeit very visible, exceptions and are not even close to being the norm. Many wealthy pastors get much of their income from music or books rather than the pulpit. Although most evangelical books do not make it to mainstream bookstores, only found in select Christian locations, they still account for one-third of the commercial books sold in the United States.[125]

As for the alleged suppression of true Christianity, to put it politely, the claims and charges far exceed the evidence. These claims have been around for a long time. Generally, they take the following form,

> The leaders of the church (normally the Catholic Church is singled out) at one of the church councils got together and removed all the parts of the Bible that they didn't like. They then rewrote the sections of the Bible that remained to suit their own needs. If only we had the original Bible before it

124 Leo Roster, *Religions of America* (New York: Simon and Schuster, 1975) p. 461
125 John Naisbitt, *Megatrends* (New York: Warner Books, 1982) p. 240

changed, we could see that Christ truly taught certain doctrines.

The particular doctrine supposedly removed or changed depends on the group making the claim. For example, with the rise of the New Age movement in the 1970s to 1990s, adherences claimed that the early Church Fathers removed reincarnation. The more recent popular novel and movie *The Da Vinci Code* claimed that the councils changed the role of women.

The main problem with these claims is that, as detailed in the first book in this series, there is no evidence that any of these changes occurred, and there is strong evidence that they did not. Thus, at best, these claims would be pure speculation.

A hundred years ago, it may have been conceivable to hold that such changes occurred, at least as a possibility. Now, this is no longer a viable position. With the discoveries made in the last hundred years, the evidence strongly argues against any such changes. There is virtually no doubt that the text of the Bible we have today is, for all practical purposes, identical to that written down by the apostles and prophets.[126]

The Early Church

The church councils were not gatherings that rewrote the Bible. Instead, they were meeting to formally agree on Christianity's central doctrines. Growth and persecution marked the early years of the church.

During this period, the church was not an organized group with a clearly defined leadership structure, like some denominations today. Instead, the church was a group of independent bodies loosely linked by similar beliefs.

This all began to change in A.D. 312 with the conversion of the Roman Emperor Constantine to the Christian faith.[127] Constantine

126 See *Evidence for the Bible, Consider Christianity Series, Volume 1*, Chapter One.

127 Some have questioned if Constantine's conversion was truly a heart

made Christianity the favored religion of the Empire. Constantine wanted to bring order and unity to the church as both an Emperor and a Christian. So, he played an important role in settling some of the disputes.

One of the earliest controversies started in A.D. 318 between Bishop Alexander, the Bishop of the City of Alexandria in Egypt, and one of his Senior Presbyters, Arius. In his attempt to understand the relationship between the Father and the Son, Arius took the position that the Son was not, in reality, God and that Jesus was inferior to the Father.

This view is not in agreement with the teachings of the Bible. However, Arius was a powerful speaker who could attract a following. When Arius continued teaching that Jesus was not God, the bishop excommunicated him and some of his followers. His excommunication did not end the controversy, and there arose a need for the church to set forth what was and was not acceptable doctrine.

Constantine first sent one of his advisors, Bishop Ossius, to Alexandria to settle the matter and reconcile the two factions. When this failed, Constantine called for a general gathering of the church Bishops to discuss and resolve the issue.

In the city of Nicaea, 220 bishops met for a general council of the church in A.D. 325. By the end, the Council of Nicaea produced a statement of belief that has come down to us as the Nicene Creed. Affirming the doctrine of the Trinity, the Nicene Creed settled the Arian question, at least for a time. Constantine achieved his goal of church unity, at least temporarily.

This unity was not due to the power of Constantine, for he did not have the ability to enforce any acceptance of the creed. Instead,

---

felt spiritual change, or just a shrewd political maneuver. We are taking no position on that issue. Whatever Constantine's personal relationship with God may have been, he did have a profound effects on the relationship between the Roman Empire and Christianity.

unity came because, of those bishops who had attended the council, only two refused to sign the creed when the council ended.

After the council, the creed quickly gained acceptance throughout the Christian world. The quick acceptance came because the Council of Nicaea did not create new doctrines but merely reaffirmed old doctrines as the church's official position.

Once the church had an official status within the Roman Empire, its structure began to formalize. In a process that took hundreds of years, a loose network of churches slowly emerged into what we recognize today as the Catholic Church. Through the efforts of Ambrose, the Bishop of Milan from A.D. 374 to A.D. 397, the church began to influence the emperors.

In the latter part of the fourth century, Damasus, the Bishop of Rome, began claiming the primacy of the Roman bishops over Bishops from other cities. He did this by putting forth the contention that Peter had been the foundation for the church and that the bishops of Rome could trace their authority back to Peter. Still, it was not until the latter part of the sixth century that the office of the pope as we know it today began to be established by Pope Gregory the Great.

The Church in the Middle Ages

With the fall of the Roman Empire, the status of Christianity changed once again. Many at the time, and later, blamed Christianity for the fall of the Roman Empire. Since the Renaissance, many have added the so-called Dark Ages that followed to the problems created by Christianity. According to the theory, Rome fell because Christianity,

> had destroyed the old faith that had given moral character to the Roman soul and stability to the Roman state. It had declared war upon the classic culture – upon science, philosophy, literature, and art. It had brought an enfeebling oriental mysticism into the realistic stoicism of Roman life; it had turned men's thoughts from the tasks of this world to an

enervating preparation for some cosmic catastrophe, and had lured them into seeking individual salvation through asceticism and prayer, rather than the collective salvation through devotion to the state. It disrupted the unity of the Empire, while soldier and emperors were struggling to preserve it; it had discouraged its adherents from holding office, or rendering military service; it had preached an ethic of nonresistance and peace when the survival of the Empire had demanded a will to war. Christ's victory had been Rome's death.[128]

While this view was once popular among earlier historians, as our understanding of the decline and fall of the Roman Empire grew, it became untenable. The roots of many problems started before Christianity. Actually, it is far more likely that "the growth of Christianity was more an effect than a cause of Rome's decay."[129]

Whatever the causes, one thing is clear: Rome's fall created a power vacuum filled by the church as the last remaining institution. The church's bishops, not the Roman authorities, often negotiated with the barbarian invaders.[130]

As we saw earlier, many see the church's role in this period as ushering in the so-called Dark Ages. Renaissance Humanists originated this view as they saw themselves as restorers of what had been in the Classical period, a golden age destroyed by the superstitions of the church.

This view of the church is still prevalent today. You can hear it in the often repeated charge by skeptics that to allow an influence of religion is to risk a return to the Dark Ages.

I heard a professor of history sum up the main problem with this view. When asked, 'When were the Dark Ages?' His answer was simple, "They never existed."

---

128 Will Durant, *Caesar and Christ*, (New York, Simon and Schuster, 1944) p. 667
129 Durant, *Caesar*, p. 667
130 E. Glen Hinson, *The Early Church: Origins to the Dawn of the Middle Ages*, (Nashville, Tn, Abingdon, 1996) p. 272

The idea they did came from the self-serving view of the Renaissance Humanists who tried to elevate their own role by downplaying those in what historians now refer to as the Middle Ages.

While the roots of Rome's fall are complex, its immediate cause is not: several groups like the Ostrogoths, Visigoths, and Vandals overran Rome in the barbarian invasions. These invasions brought about the collapse of government order. As the historian Will Durant noted,

> The basic cause of cultural retrogression was not Christianity but barbarism; not religion but war. The human inundations ruined or impoverished cities, monasteries, libraries, schools, and made impossible the life of the scholar or the scientist. Perhaps the destruction would have been worse had not the Church maintained some measure of order in a crumbling civilization.[131]

With the collapse of the Roman Civilization, the Church was, in many ways, the last remaining vestige of that civilization.

> The Germanic invasions dealt a devastating blow to culture and learning on the edges of the empire but even there it survived, thanks especially to the monasteries and the churches. Monks copied and illuminated precious manuscripts. Monasteries built up libraries to preserve the treasures of the past, both classical and Christian, Monastic schools perpetuated the tradition of learning.[132]

The Middle Ages resulted in a mixture of three components: the dying Roman civilization, the church, and the barbarism of the invading tribes. The church's influence was more than just a continuance of Roman civilization; it was a distinct change.

> For the first time in European history the teachers of mankind preached an ethic of kindliness, obedience, humility, patience, mercy, purity, chastity, and tenderness – virtues ... admirably adapted to restore order to a de-moral-ized people,

---

131 Will Durant, *The Age of Faith*, (New York, Simon and Schuster, 1950) p. 79
132 Hinson, *Early* p. 306

to tame the marauding barbarian, to moderate the violence of a falling world.[133]

Still, the influence went both ways. As the church sought to transform the barbarian, the barbarian was also changing the church and the social structures of Rome. The resulting mixture of Christian, Roman, and barbarian cultures resulted in the culture of the Middle Ages.

Another problem during the Middle Ages was Rome's fall, which left control over much of society in the hands of the clergy. As a result, the church was the only institution of any real prestige or power left in Western Europe during much of this period.

People seeking power and influence, who before would have entered governmental positions, instead entered the church. As a result, church leadership positions were often not given based on spiritual qualifications, as much as political infighting or bribes.

Rome's fall also increased the existing tensions between the church in Rome and Constantinople. With the fall of Rome, Constantinople became the center of wealth and political power. Although in the process of political decline, Rome still considered itself the head of the entire church and, thus, the center of spiritual power. This division in power led to an ever-increasing split between the two cities.

The churches in the East tended to see church power as resting in a council of bishops from the most important cities. The Western Church, led by Rome, saw power as centered in the bishop of Rome, the Pope.

As the West declined, communication became more complicated, and the divisions became even more pronounced. In the sixth century, the emperor Justinian changed the official language of the Eastern Empire from Latin to Greek. As a result, a language barrier further separated the Eastern and Western churches.

The divisions between the Eastern and Western churches came to a head in A.D. 1054 when Pope Leo IX sent a delegation led by

133 Will Durant, *The Age of Faith*, (New York, Simon and Schuster, 1950) p. 76

Humbert of Moyenmoutier to Constantinople. The delegation demanded that the Eastern churches submit to the authority of Rome. Leo excommunicated the Patriarchs who led the Eastern Churches when they refused, causing the first of many splits.

The split divided the universal church into two main groups of local churches. The churches in the East became the Eastern Orthodox Church, while those in the West became the Roman Catholic Church. In the West, the Roman Catholic Church was the primary source of power and influence throughout much of Europe.

The Crusades

The popular view of the Crusades is that they were an attempt to spread the Christian faith through conquest and war. While this view undoubtedly has some truth, the facts are a little more complex.

Since its founding in the seventh century, Islam has spread through war. Mohammed is the only founder of a major religion to have been a military leader. While in Medina, "he planned sixty-five campaigns and raids, and personally led twenty-seven of them."[134]

As such, it is unsurprising that his followers followed his example, conquering Arabia, eastward to Persia and India, westward into Egypt, North Africa, and up into Spain. Their attempts to expand into Europe through Spain ended after a week-long battle in 732 near Tours.

To the east, in 1063, Alp Arslan became Seljuq sultan at the death of his uncle. He went on to conquer Herat, Armenia, Georgia, and Syria. In 1071, his forces had a significant victory over the Byzantine army at the battle of Manzikert.[135]

This defeat left Constantinople vulnerable. Less than twenty years after the split between the Eastern and Western churches,

---

134 Will Durant, *The Age of Faith*, (New York, Simon and Schuster, 1950) p. 170

135 Will Durant, *The Age of Faith*, (New York, Simon and Schuster, 1950) p. 308

the Byzantine Empire was threatened with an invasion and was in danger of falling.

At the same time, the Western Empire was experiencing almost the exact opposite problem. Europe had a growing population and a system of inheritance that gave all property to the firstborn. This system left others without a source of income.

The result was many men for whom war was the best hope for wealth and advancement. Unfortunately, at least for those seeking wealth and advancement, very few enemies needed fighting. This left many knights roaming the countryside looking for fights and, as one would expect, causing a lot of problems.

In an attempt to deal with the problem, the church in France proclaimed what was called the *Peace of God*. This peace attempted to persuade these knights not to kill civilians. Later, a *Truce of God* was also declared in an attempt to at least stop the fighting on holy days. In 1095, Pope Urban II was to appear before a council in Clermont, France, to encourage this effort.

A short time before the council met, a delegation from Alexius Comnenus, the Byzantine emperor, met with Pope Urban II to request assistance against the Turkish forces threatening him. All indications are that Comnenus simply wanted a few mercenaries to bolster his troops.

Urban, however, saw a chance to kill several birds with but a single stone. By calling a crusade to free the Holy Land, the immediate response would give all the knights currently wandering the countryside and causing problems, something to do. Even more importantly, it would give them somewhere else to do it.

Urban II also hoped that sending such a large force to the Middle East would demonstrate the superiority and leadership of the Roman Church. This would help persuade the Eastern Church to return.

A third reason was to embarrass the German Emperor Henry VII. A short time before this, Henry VII forced the pope to flee Rome. By calling a crusade to defend the Holy Land that excluded the Germans, Urban could demonstrate his role as leader and bashed Henry, all at the same time.

So, at a council for peace, Urban called for a great crusade to 'free the Holy Land from the Infidels.' The call was far more popular than Urban intended.

It was a time when religious pilgrimages were very popular. The perceived threat to such pilgrimages to the Holy Land struck a cord among the people. Popular preachers soon spread the call for a crusade. What Urban had intended as a call for knights, many quickly perceived as a call for everyone.

Before the first Crusade could start, many smaller bands set out on their own for the Holy Land. Led by popular religious figures, such as Peter the Hermit, these bands were poorly organized and ill-equipped. Many never reached the Holy Land.

Those who did, did so by looting and pillaging the villages they passed through. Many did not even wait to get to the Holy Land to begin their "war for God" but began attacking and killing every Jew they could find.

Those groups who finally made it to Constantinople quickly began to cause problems there as well. Emperor Alexius dealt with these troublemakers by sending them into battle without waiting for the first crusaders to arrive, whereby the Turks quickly slaughtered them.

When the first Crusade finally arrived, it 'freed the Holy Land,' yet their success was short-lived. In less than fifty years, the Turks recaptured the northern city of Edessa. The second Crusade to retake this territory was not successful. Neither was the third or fourth Crusades, which attempted to win back the City of Jerusalem, recaptured by Egypt in 1197. In 1291, the last Western outpost fell, and the Crusades ended.

Peaks and Valleys

The power of the popes peaked in the early part of the thirteenth century with the rule of Pope Innocent III. During his term as pope, Innocent III obtained the submission of both the Kings of France and England. In the case of England, Innocent III had the power to declare the throne vacant in 1209 until King John agreed to submit to the will of the Roman Church.

This power, which the popes could wield even over kings, faded after Innocent's death. Less than a hundred years later, the balance of power had shifted to such an extent that France could force the election of the Archbishop of Bordeaux to become Pope Clement V.

The King of France controlled Clement so much that he never even went to Rome. Instead, he ruled from the city of Avignon in the south of France. The subsequent six popes also ruled from France in what is now called the Avignon Captivity.

After seventy years of French domination, things went from bad to worse for the church. In 1378, Pope Gregory XI returned the papacy to Rome shortly before his death. Pope Urban VI was then elected as a compromise candidate who would stay in Rome. Urban's election restored order to the church for a short time. Then Urban offended the king of France, demanding he submit to his authority.

Instead of submitting, France used its power to form a new council of bishops, immediately declaring Urban's election invalid. The council then elected a French Pope, Clement VII.

Not too surprisingly, Clement returned the papacy to Avignon. While this seemed to fix things for France, there was a minor problem; Urban did not accept the new council's decision and continued to rule from Rome.

Both popes promptly excommunicated each other, and the countries of Europe began to take sides. This state of affairs continued through the next forty years and several sets of popes, with both sides holding their councils and electing their popes.

In an attempt to settle the issue once and for all, a group of cardinals met in the city of Pisa in 1409. Their solution was simple: they removed both popes and then elected a new one in their place, Alexander V.

Yet, instead of having the desired effect, Alexander was quickly rejected by the Roman and the Avignon popes, leaving the Roman Catholic Church with three popes, all claiming to be the church's head.

Eventually, the problem was settled by a similar plan to the one proposed by the Council of Bishops at Pisa. The result was the subsequent election of a single pope, Martin V, in 1417. This episode demonstrates how much the church had fallen under the control of Kings and how they used the church as a tool to carry out their wishes.

The Inquisition

During the first five centuries of the Middle Ages, apart from the ongoing power struggle between the eastern and western halves of the church, Christianity was seldom challenged in any significant theological sense, at least not internally. The church felt safe.

In ancient Greek and Roman law, death was the maximum punishment for heresy. Still, in the eleventh century, Pope Leo IX held that the maximum punishment for heresy should be ex-communication from the church.[136]

In the twelfth century, a rising tide of anticlericalism began to change this. Sadly, as with most groups, the more those in the church felt threatened, the less inclined they were to tolerate opposition.

In 1088, something new started in Bologna, Italy, with the founding of the oldest continuously operating university in the world. One of the early research subjects was Roman law, resulting in a revival. Under Roman law, a person suspected of heresy when no one would testify could result in an *inquisiti*.

During an *inquisiti*, a judge questioned the accused to assess the validity of the charges. Roman law also permitted the use of torture to get confessions. The combination of rising threats to the

---

136 Will Durant, *The Age of Faith*, (New York, Simon and Schuster, 1950) p. 777

church and the reintroduction of Roman law laid the framework for the Inquisition.[137]

At first, the Inquisition did not use torture. Then, in 1252, Innocent IV allowed its use in limited circumstances. Over time, this was expanded, eventually including even witnesses.

As corruption grew within the church, those running the Inquisition, at times, became more interested in the gold it acquired in fines and penalties than the faith it supposedly was trying to protect.

Critics have greatly exaggerated the number killed in the Inquisition, and I have heard claims that it killed millions. Such numbers are unfounded. In fact, detailed investigations by historians have tended to revise down the much less excessive numbers of earlier historians.

For example, Bernard de Caux was considered a zealous inquisitor who tried many cases. None of his cases ended with the accused sentenced to death. Out of 930 heretics condemned by Bernard Gui, only 45 received the death penalty.[138] The infamous Spanish Inquisition may have killed as many as 2,000 people—horrible, but not millions.

The Reformation

During this period, the corruption within the church continued to expand and grow deeper. Practices that at one time started from good motives became corrupt. An excellent example of this was the practice of selling indulgences.[139] Originally, indulgences began as a way for the church to recognize the participation of those unable to go to the Crusades but who could support them financially.

137 Will Durant, *The Age of Faith*, (New York, Simon and Schuster, 1950) p. 777, 781
138 Will Durant, *The Age of Faith*, (New York, Simon and Schuster, 1950) p. 783
139 I am not endorsing the theology behind indulgences, for I do not think that the practice is in accordance with the Bible. All I am saying is that even though the theology is bad, the practice was started with good motives.

When the church began to decline from its position of power and influence, so did revenues. Before long, some within the church saw indulgences as little more than an easy way to raise money. At times of financial need, those in charge would appoint people to go from town to town, like traveling salesmen of salvation holding large rallies to sell indulgences.

Corruption extended throughout the church hierarchy. By the time of the Reformation, it was commonplace for prospective bishops to have to pay large sums of money to gain their positions. Often, this would leave them with large debts. There was basically only one source of income for a bishop: the people to whom they were supposed to minister.

This is not to say that all in the church were corrupt and power-hungry. Many, especially those at the lower levels, were very dedicated to serving the Lord and did their best to resist this corruption. Sometimes, going up against the church hierarchy cost them their lives.

Throughout the Renaissance, many groups saw the corruption existing throughout the church and called for reform. In the spring of 1517, all the forces for change came together.

In 1515, Albrecht of Brandenburg, with a lot of political maneuvering and bribes, obtained the archbishopric of Mainz. His success left Albrecht with significant debt, mainly to the House of Fugger.

At about the same time, Pope Leo X needed money to complete St. Peter's Basilica in Rome. Leo and Abrecht were close allies, so they devised a plan to sell indulgences and split the money; Albrecht to pay his debts, and the pope to build St. Peter's.

To sell the indulgences, Leo and Albrecht hired one of the best salesmen in the business, a Dominican friar named Johann Tetzel. So, throughout the spring of 1517, Tetzel sold indulgences around Wittenberg.

This enraged a young priest in the area so much that he began preparing a response to this practice. His response took the form of a list of 95 points. Following the standard method for starting a debate for the period, on October 31, 1517, Martin Luther nailed his list to the church door in Wittenberg. In the process, he started the Reformation.

Although Luther did not intend to break away from the Roman Catholic Church, the results of his actions are well known. Luther was not the first to protest, but he was the first to succeed.

The reason for his success rests largely with forces outside of the church. The most important of these were the recent invention of the printing press and the political tension in Germany at the time.

When Luther started his protest, many in Germany were looking for a way to break with Emperor Charles V. Since Charles had the blessing of the church in Rome, Luther provided just such an excuse, for breaking with the church in Rome was to break with Charles.

For the most part, the Reformation gave the church back to the people by taking power away from the hierarchy. It also started the shift towards the individual and, thus, was a key precursor for the enlightenment that would begin a hundred years later.

Still, the reformation had its problems. With no central authority to settle theological disputes, divisions between groups quickly resulted in new churches or denominations. Because of this, the history of Protestantism, those "protesting" the Roman Church, is marked by an ever-increasing number of denominations.

An emphasis on the Bible also marked Protestantism. The Roman Catholic Church bases its theology on the Bible, the traditions of the Church, and, in exceptional cases, the pope's statements. Protestantism sees the Bible as the only source.

This difference in focus is why, at many Protestant services, the main focus is teaching the Bible. The pastor gives the sermon from the center of the church. At Roman Catholic services, the teaching of the Scripture is secondary, and communion is the main focus. Thus, Catholics put the Alar on which the sacrifice of the

Cross is made present in the center, and the priest gives the sermon or homily from the side.

The conflict between the Catholics and Protestants was frequently more than mere theological disputes. Often, they were as much political as religious and military rather than scholarly.

The Thirty Years' War was the most notable and destructive of the religious wars of this period. It devastated much of Germany from 1618 to 1648. Yet even here, the causes are mixed.

Nothing reveals this more clearly than with the signing of the Treaty of Prague in 1635, "the religious question disappeared from the war." Yet, the war and its devastation continued for another thirteen years, and these were some of the worst of the war.

Period of Revival

The centuries that followed the Reformation were a time of great ferment and unrest. Periods of revival and competition among the many divergent groups were commonplace. The newly discovered land of America provided a new opportunity to live with religious freedom. As a result, many people left Europe to settle in the New World.

Others came to America as missionaries. The commonly held view that a missionary was someone who oppressed and forced Christianity upon the helpless inhabitants of the New World is a gross distortion. Although there is some truth to this view, more often than not, the missionary stood between the Native Americans and those who wished to exploit them.[140]

Unfortunately, the god of gold often won out over the God of the Bible. "Missionaries caught in the complex of national ambitions sometimes surrendered to political demands; more frequently ... they lessened brutality and widened charity."[141] Some gave their lives in the attempt.

---

140 Edwin Scott Gaustad, *A Religious History of America*, (New York, Harper and Row, 1974) pg 11
141 Gaustad, *Religious*, pg 17

The churches' slow but steady movement away from governmental influences also marked this period. The church and the state struggle has always been a two-way street. Today, it is commonplace to hear about the problems caused by religion interfering with government. Historically, religion has been used as much, if not more, by governments trying to reach their own goals.

Many of the early settlers coming to America were fleeing religiously oppressive governments. These governments used religion in many ways; one was as a means to justify their rule with *The Divine Right of Kings*. This belief meant that if you disagreed with the state religion, you also disagreed with how the king justified his rule. That could be dangerous.

Since the Reformation, there has been an ever-increasing, albeit slow, process of reform marked by periods of revival. These religious revivals changed individuals and society, as many Christians renewed their faith in God and sought to change their lives. This was nothing new. From its earliest days, as Christ transformed individuals, those individuals went on to impact the society in which they lived.

For example, because of their reverence for all human life, early Christians ended the practice of infanticide that had existed in Roman society. Under Roman law, the Father had the right of life and death over his children. If a father did not want a child for any reason, such as a girl when he only wanted sons, the child could be taken outside the city and left for wild animals. Early Christians would save these children and raise them themselves.

You can see this same transformational process in the great revivals that swept England and America during the eighteenth century. During these revivals, many people's lives dramatically changed.

One such convert was the slave trader John Newton. He is probably best known for writing hymns such as *Amazing Grace* following his conversion. Newton did not restrict his new faith solely to his personal life but became a strong advocate for the abolition of slavery. He also significantly influenced William Wilberforce.

Wilberforce was a member of Parliament at the time of his conversion to Christianity in 1784-5. Before his conversion, Wilberforce had taken very little interest in the issue of slavery. Because of his newfound faith, and with Newton's encouragement, Wilberforce soon became one of the foremost leaders in the movement to outlaw slavery in England. This was a fight that occupied Wilberforce for almost fifty years.

Wilberforce's religious motivations were obvious and noted by his opposition. In 1788, while speaking in opposition to a law supported by Wilberforce that would have ended the slave trade in England, Lord Melbourne complained that "Things have come to a pretty pass when religion is allowed to invade public life."[142] Finally, in 1833, one month after the death of Wilberforce, the *Slavery Abolition Act* was passed.

As in England, Christian ethics strongly influenced the Abolitionist movement in the United States. Many circuit preachers like Peter Cartwright preached both the word of God and the abolition of slavery.

Elijah Lovejoy was a Presbyterian pastor and the editor of the religious newspaper, *St. Louis Observer*. Lovejoy used his position as editor to condemn slavery every chance he got.

The pressure against him became so great it forced Lovejoy to move his press to Alto, Illinois. The persecution did not stop, and Lovejoy's presses were destroyed three times in a single year. Still, Lovejoy would not give in and continued his strong opposition to slavery. On November 7, 1837, a mob attacked Lovejoy's paper for a fourth time, killing Lovejoy in the process.

Throughout the church's history, Christians were not only active in social issues but took it for granted that they would be. Whether it was the early church's fight to stop infanticide or the fight for the

---

142 Herbert Schlossberg and Marvin Olasky, *Turning Point: A Christian World View Declaration* (Westchester, Ill: Crossway Books, 1987) p. 116

abolition of slavery in the eighteenth and nineteenth centuries, it was typical for the church to take an active role in social issues. By the end of the eighteenth century, this attitude began to change.

The Origins of the Modern Church

The church has never existed in a vacuum, and the society around it has always influenced it. Since the Renaissance, Western civilization has been putting an ever greater emphasis on the material world, with a corresponding decrease in interest in the spiritual. By the middle of the eighteenth century, much of society began to ignore the spiritual side of people's nature.

This change in emphasis from the spiritual to the material resulted in a dispute within the church over what has come to be called the Personal vs. Social Gospel controversy. The personal gospel emphasizes the conversion of the individual. Once saved, then you can deal with any problems that may exist in their lives. The social gospel, strongly influenced by the new science of sociology, emphasized eliminating the problems in a person's life. You can focus on salvation once you care for a person's problems.

The Bible teaches that physical and spiritual needs are important and that the church should strike a balance between the two. During the eighteenth century, as society devalued the spiritual for the material, so did some parts of the church.

The severe social problems created by the Industrial Revolution further accelerated this shift toward the material. When the dispute between personal and social gospels developed into a controversy, rather than moving back to a more balanced position, the two camps polarized the issue, widening the gap even further.

At about the same time, another movement, liberalism, began to take hold of many of the mainline denominations. Throughout the church's history, there have always been those who have not believed in the Gospel.

With Rationalism's rise, it became popular in many intellectual circles to attack the Bible and its teachings as something that

belonged to the superstitious past. One stumbling block prevent-
ed these criticisms from taking hold in popular culture, and this
stumbling block was our very existence. How did we get here if
God didn't create us?

Although the concept of biological evolution had existed for
centuries, it did not have the scientific underpinnings to allow it to
be called anything more than an interesting idea. This all changed
on November 24, 1859, when Charles Darwin published *The Origin
of Species by Means of Natural Selection or the Preservation of Favored
Races in the Struggle for Life.*

Darwin took the idea of evolution and placed it on a scientific
footing. Although the theory remained untested at many vital
points, it was quickly accepted by rationalists and extended to explain not only the existence of animals but also human beings. So
significant was the impact of Darwin's *The Origin of Species* that it
has been called,

> one of the most important [books] ever written. No other
> modern work has done so much to change man's concept of
> himself and of the universe in which he lives... The usual at-
> tempts to explain the nature of life, the diversity of living things,
> their marvelous adaptations, and other fundamental aspects,
> of the living world were still metaphysical, at best, and often
> frankly supernatural... *The Origin of Species* changed all that.[143]

The concept of evolution swept through the intellectual community like wildfire. People began to apply evolution as a concept
to all sorts of things. If people have evolved, then why not the things
that people create? Evolutionary theories soon began appearing for
society as a whole.

It was to be less than a hundred years before the world would
become engulfed in a world war to stop some of these theories.
Although Darwin did not intend it, Hitler's concept of a Master

---

143 Note the implicit rejection of the supernatural in this statement as was
discussed in the earlier chapters of this book. George Gaylord Simpson, in
Forward to *Origin of Species* (New York: Collier, 1962) p. 5

Race that should rule over and dominate those considered inferior traces its philosophical roots directly back through the now-discarded science of eugenics to Darwin's *The Origin of Species* and his idea of survival of the fittest.

Religion did not escape this attempt to force everything into a rationalistic and evolutionary framework. Later in the nineteenth century, theories about how religion evolved became popular. These theories left no room for God or the supernatural.

Since the Bible did not fit into this new and modern way of approaching religion, the Bible had to be "adjusted" to fit. Scholars developed elaborate theories using the latest "scientific" advances as they attempted to show that the Bible was nothing more than the creation of people.

For many, the Bible was religious theories that people had written down, collected, or edited to fit the needs of the moment. According to these new theories, Moses did not receive the first five books of the Bible from God; they were compiled later from myths.

The prophet Isaiah could not have given a prophecy about the nation of Israel being in captivity because that happened after he died. A second Isaiah must have written them during or after the Babylonian captivity.

Similarly, the scientific approach to the Bible claimed to have shown that the Gospels could not have been written by Matthew, Mark, Luke, and John because these Gospels were written long after these people had died.

Claims like these came with ever-increasing regularity and forced the church to take a stand. The question was often: Is the Bible correct, or is science correct?

Those in the church who accepted such modern views concerning religion and the Bible were called liberals, though not to be confused with political liberals, and their theories are grouped under the heading of liberalism.

As some in the universities and seminaries of the mainline denominations began teaching these liberal theories, bitter battles arose for control. Many quickly realized that those who controlled the seminaries training future pastors would also control the church in a few years.

Battles for the control of seminaries marked the beginning of the twentieth century. Since those defending the Bible were, for the most part, unfamiliar with the ways of science, they did not know how to respond. By the end of the 1920s, the battles were essentially over, with liberalism controlling many mainline seminaries.

In response to liberalism, a new movement called fundamentalism was born. The fundamentalists believed strongly that the Bible was the word of God. Not only was it inspired, it was also inerrant. They felt that the church needed to stress the fundamentals of the faith. The personal vs. social gospel controversy also entered into this movement, with the fundamentalists coming out strongly favoring the personal gospel.

The liberalism and personal vs. social gospel controversies have left lasting marks on the church that have only recently begun to fade. Because of liberalism's takeover of many Christian universities, some fundamentalists saw universities themselves as the enemy. After all, this was where many attacks on Christianity originated.

Over time, this distrust of some universities, combined with the general anti-Christian bias that was, and still is, present in most universities, turned into a general distrust of all schools. Today, it is still not difficult to find churches whose pastors have no formal training in the Bible.

In fact, until recently, some churches viewed going to college as something to be done only at significant risk. Another group, Evangelicals, are theologically very similar to fundamentalists, but they never adopted the fundamentalist's anti-intellectual stance.

The personal vs. social gospel controversy has also had its effect. Many fundamentalists and evangelicals saw any involvement with social issues as a wasted effort when the real problem was the need for Christ. Personal witnessing and salvation became a Christian's sole duty to their fellow human beings.

The result was an almost total withdrawal from society for many Christians. They tried to have as little to do with society as possible except for witnessing.

Since fundamentalists and evangelicals stress the personal and transforming nature of salvation, described as being "Born Again," both groups are often referred to as Born-Again Christians (John 3:3-8). This became a popular term in the 1970s and 80s.

Another significant church controversy around the turn of the 20th century was the gifts of the Holy Spirit. The church's historical position has been that the gifts of the Holy Spirit are given to believers when the Spirit chooses.

Around the turn of the century, some churches began to stress some gifts, specifically speaking in tongues, in highly emotional services. Many of these churches taught that all believers should speak in tongues.

Other churches reacted by proclaiming that the Holy Spirit no longer gives these gifts as they were for an early age and prohibited their use. Today, those who stress the active use of gifts like tongues are referred to as charismatics, and they can be found in most denominations.

The Church Today

By the early 1960s, the more fundamentalist portions of the church had retreated almost entirely into its own subculture. Since the larger culture generally agreed with fundamental Christian values, a sort of "you don't bother us, we won't bother you" situation developed.

For example, for many fundamentalists, politics was a dirty word, something of the world in which Christians didn't get involved. Many did not even get involved enough to vote; it wasn't their concern.

The 1960s also began some major upheavals in society and the church. The government was getting bigger and starting to encroach into the realm of the church. More importantly, the government's attitude towards religion was increasingly hostile.

While most people remained religious, some cultural elites used the courts with great success to transform the fundamental nature of the American culture into one completely secular. The founding fathers wrote The First Amendment to protect religion. In the 1960s, the Supreme Court reinterpreted it as the primary tool to restrict religion and drive it from the public square.

Much of this battle has taken place in the schools. Bible reading and prayer in the classroom were banned. The Court then extended the ban to include sporting events and graduations. Christmas and Easter breaks became winter and spring breaks.

Textbooks even changed the history of Thanksgiving. The Pilgrims became non-religious: people who take long journeys. At the first Thanksgiving, the pilgrims thanked the Indians instead of God.

Perhaps of even more concern, rather than the traditional morality, schools replaced this with a new, more value-neutral approach. Many Christians saw this as directly undermining the moral values they believed in and were trying to teach their children. The net result of these and other societal changes was that the subculture of the more traditional Christians was becoming harder to maintain.

Churches themselves were also changing. After decades of growth, since the sixties, most of the traditional mainline denominations, which were increasingly dominated by liberal theology, have seen a steady decline in church attendance.

> By 1990 these denominations had lost between one-fifth and one-third of the membership they claimed in 1965 and the proportion of Americans affiliated with them had reached a twentieth-century low.[144]

Yet, while mainline churches were in a long period of decline, many more theologically conservative churches were experiencing explosive growth. These changes began making headlines in the

144 Benton Johnson, Dean R. Hoge & Donald A. Luidens, *Mainline Churches: The Real Reason for Decline. First Things*, 31 (March 1993): 13-18

seventies with the Jesus Movement and President Carter, who, while running for office, said that he had been "Born Again." The Jesus Movement resulted in many new "denominations" appearing overnight.

The first real social change began with a new attitude toward school. Some Christians and many others felt that public schools were no longer a suitable place to send their children. As a result, churches began to establish their own schools.

Starting with grade schools, then adding junior high and then high schools, some churches now offer complete K-12 schooling. These schools are often as good as or better than that provided through the public school system.

Today, it is possible for a child to go from preschool through college in many majors, such as Journalism, Law, Psychology, and Business, to mention just a few, and never leave a church-run school. With this current emphasis on education, the anti-intellectual sentiment of the earlier part of the century rapidly disappeared among many fundamental Christians.

Over the last several decades, whether they liked it or not, conservative Christians were being thrust into society. Also disappearing was their feeling that Christians should not get involved in politics.

Until the 1980s, these Christians were so uninvolved that they did not register in public opinion polls. This phenomenon could be seen during Pat Robertson's presidential campaign when many pollsters complained that Robertson's people "just did not show up."

Yet, as the country moves farther and farther away from biblical principles and the government keeps expanding its influence, more traditional Christians are becoming concerned. With each new issue, be it a court ruling that the Pledge of Allegiance was unconstitutional because it mentions "under God" or a court imposing same-sex marriage, more Christians became concerned.

Since the second edition's publication, this has only become even more pronounced. Many churches changed their by-laws and practices in the last ten years to protect themselves from government action.

Some Christians have even found themselves in court for trying to live by their beliefs, though the Supreme Court has tended to side with them. Still, not everyone can afford to take their fight to the Supreme Court.

Equally as dramatic have been the changes in the Church in the rest of the world. The decline in church attendance throughout most of Western Europe has been far more pronounced than in the mainline churches in the US. For all intent and purposes, Western Europe is now well into a post-Christian phase in its history.

This decline was more than offset by continuing strength in Latin America and strong growth in Africa and Asia. Christianity is no longer just a European religion.

Conclusion

As we have seen, the Christian church is not a perfect institution. It has its faults and problems. Throughout history, the church as an institution has been a force for great good but also great evil.

The church is an institution controlled by people. If the people who run the church seek to use it for their selfish purposes, then the church can be used to cause tremendous harm. Unfortunately, there is no assurance that those who run a church will even be Christian. Due to the encroachment of liberalism into many mainline denominations, some in leadership no longer accept all of the fundamental doctrines of Christianity defined in the last chapter.

What can be said is that the church, like any institution, is only as good as the people in it. This is not to ignore the evil done in the name of Christianity but to point out that any system involving people can be directed toward evil.

I am sure neither Charles Darwin nor Karl Marx intended evil to come from their works. Still, they planted the seeds for the greatest evils in history.

Many critics of Christianity point to the number of people killed by religion as an example of how dangerous it is. Tragically, there is some truth to this charge. As mentioned earlier, the Spanish Inquisition killed as many as 2,000 people.[145]

Still, the charge is grossly exaggerated. As terrible as these numbers are, they pale compared to those killed in the name of movements that try to ignore God. From Darwin's theory of the survival of the fittest came the science of eugenics, which helped spawn Adolph Hitler and his idea of a master race, leaving 11 million dead in concentration camps.[146]

The writings of Karl Marx resulted in Joseph Stalin and Mao Tse-tung. Historians have estimated that Stalin was responsible for between 25 to 60 million deaths.[147] Mao Tse-tung is the greatest mass murderer in the history of the world.[148]

Another charge frequently leveled by critics claims that most wars in human history are due to religion. This charge is not even close to being correct. While war and armed conflict are sadly a very common occurrence in human history, far more were caused by factors such as greed, desire for power, etc., not religion.

Most of the wars of Rome and other earlier civilizations were not due to religion, nor were the barbarian invasions that destroyed Rome. During the Middle Ages, the Church sought to exert its influence over kings to limit conflicts.

---

145 *Encyclopedia Britannica*, 15 ed., s.v. *Inquisition, Spanish*

146 The estimates for the number of people who died in the concentration camps vary considerably. That six million Jews were killed is well established, but many others also died in the camps. Estimates r.ange to has high as 25 million. see Encyclopedia Britannica, 15th ed. (1978), s.v. concentration camp

147 Mikhail Heller & Aleksandr M. Nekrich, *Utopia in Power: The History of the Soviet Union from 1917 to Present* (New York: Summit Books, 1986) p. 511

148 *The Guinness Book of Records 1992*, Mass Murder ed. Donald McFarlan (New York: Facts on File, 1991) p. 92

When this failed, it issued rules that attempted to limit the effects of war on innocent civilians. The Renaissance saw both a decline in the influence of religion and a growth in conflicts. The wars of Napoleon likewise were not religious, nor were World War I or II.

There were some religious wars, but these were the minority, and even in those, religion was rarely the sole issue. The most notable exception to this would be the wars of Islam for expansion. But this is hardly an indictment of religion in general or Christianity in specific.

The most notable exception for Christianity has been the wars between Protestants and Catholics following the Reformation. But these have been far more the exception than the rule.

When judging the church, one should also consider the principles and objectives it is to strive for and not concentrate wholly on its failures to achieve them. One should look at the Pros and the Cons instead of focusing on one or the other.

On the positive side, throughout history, the Church has been a source of tremendous good and positive social change. From its earliest days, it supported the individual and worked to improve the lives of the poor and helpless.

that "All men are created equal, that they are endowed by their Creator with certain unalienable rights," and the subsequent realization of that idea in the abolition of slavery.

When the church works to carry out the principles that Jesus Christ taught, it is a source of tremendous good. Not only are the spiritual needs of people met, but hospitals are built, the sick are cared for, the hungry fed, the naked clothed, and those in prison visited. Today, throughout the world, Christians are quietly working through their churches to care for the needs of people as they bring the Gospel of Jesus Christ.

Part II

Jesus Christ

5

Who Do You Say I Am?

Christianity is basically an historical religion. That is to say, it is not founded primarily in universal principles, but in concrete events, actual historical happenings. The most important of these is the life of a little-known Jewish carpenter.
(Huston Smith)[149]

JESUS WAS TWO years into His ministry during the late spring or early summer of A.D. 29 when He brought His disciples to the area near Caesarea Philippi. In less than a year, the Romans would crucify Him.

While there, Jesus questioned His disciples about what the people were saying about Him. The general consensus was that Jesus was a man of God, possibly even a prophet of old whom God had sent for some special mission. Then Jesus asked them, "But what about you? ...Who do you say I am" (Matthew 16:13-15)?

Central to Christianity is the question: Who is Jesus? Simon Peter best summarized the answer Christians have historically given when he responded to Jesus, "You are the Christ, the Son of the living God" (Matthew 16:15).

According to the Bible, Jesus was conceived miraculously and born to the Virgin Mary in the city of Bethlehem. He was taken to Egypt by His parents to avoid persecution by King Herod. After

---

149 Huston Smith, *The Religions of Man* (New York: Harper & Row, 1986) p. 410

Herod died in 4 B.C., Jesus returned to Judea with his parents, who settled in the city of Nazareth.

The Gospels say little concerning His childhood, except that when He was twelve years old, He was taken to Jerusalem by His parents. While in Jerusalem, Jesus amazed the teachers in the temple with His knowledge of God.

In the movie *The Last Temptation of Christ*, Jesus is portrayed as a confused man who does not know His true mission in life. Nothing could be farther from the truth. Even at the early age of twelve, Jesus already knew His identity and mission.

While in Jerusalem, Jesus became separated from His parents. After much searching, His parents finally found Him in the temple. When asked why He had remained behind, Jesus replied, "Why were you searching for me? ...Didn't you know I had to be in my Father's house?" (Luke 2:49)

Nothing else is said about Jesus until He began His ministry at about thirty. Some call the period from age twelve to thirty the lost years of Jesus. They claim that during this time, Jesus traveled to Persia to visit the magi who had visited Him.

Others claim that Jesus traveled to Tibet to learn from Buddhist monks. Still, other legends claim that Jesus traveled to Egypt and Greece. There is even a claim that Jesus traveled to Britain with Joseph of Arimathea and established a church there.

The main problem with all of these claims is that the earliest accounts of these trips do not begin appearing until hundreds of years after the completion of the Bible. By this time, Christianity was already a large and established religion.

Some of these sources are known forgeries, and others simply remain questionable. In short, no solid evidence supports any of these claims. Most likely, Jesus spent these years learning carpentry, or more likely, the building trade, from His father, Joseph, and studying the Scriptures.

When Jesus was about thirty years old, John the Baptist baptized Him. Over the next three and a half years, He gathered disciples, taught about the Kingdom of God, did many miracles, and even claimed to be God.

As His ministry grew, so did the opposition. Finally, while on a trip to Jerusalem to celebrate the Passover, Jesus was betrayed by one of those in His inner circle. He was convicted in a trial before the Sanhedrin and handed over to the Romans for crucifixion. After Jesus' death, His disciples scattered in fear for their lives.

Yet it was not over. On the following Sunday morning, Christ appeared to Mary Magdalene. Later, on the same day, He appeared to ten of His disciples. Thomas was not present and refused to believe the reports of the resurrection. This reaction forever earned him the title "doubting Thomas."

His disbelief was only temporary; one week later, Jesus appeared again. This time, all of the disciples, including Thomas, were present. Over forty days, Jesus appeared to many different people, and once, He appeared to a group of over 500. After forty days, Jesus ascended into heaven, where He will remain until the end times.

This is the Jesus of the Bible, God incarnate, who died for the sins of the world. While this is the Christian position, what do the critics say? If Jesus was not God incarnate, who was He?

The critics are divided, with their views ranging from believing that Jesus was a con artist to denying that a person named Jesus ever existed. There are many variations between these two extremes. Perhaps the most popular one is that Jesus was simply a good teacher whose disciples were a little overzealous in their descriptions of Him.

The Critic's Jesus

One of the most extreme views concerning Jesus is that there never was a Jesus of Nazareth. According to this theory, all references to Jesus were complete fabrications of the early Christian church.

While this view was prevalent during the nineteenth century, it has lost much of its support over the years. Michael Martin, a recent supporter of this view, admits that this view "is highly controversial and not widely accepted."[150] The French historian Charles Guignebert sums up the position by saying:

> Radical criticism of the traditional evidence concerning the existence of Jesus is based upon two main contentions, which have been restated by Bruno Bauer: (1) Contemporary Jewish and pagan literature makes no mention of Jesus; (2) The New Testament writings, with their inconsistencies and contradictions, their obvious interpolations and their amazing improbabilities, cannot be regarded as a trustworthy historical source.[151]

Similar to the belief that Jesus did not exist is the view that, while there may indeed have been a religious reformer named Jesus who the Romans crucified, any similarity between the historical Jesus and the Jesus found in the Gospel ends there. A popular version states that Christianity, as we now know it, did not originate with Jesus but with the apostle Paul.

According to one recent variation, Paul was a very ambitious young man. Somehow, though, Paul's career within the existing religious establishment was sidetracked and reached a dead end.

In order to make his mark on the world, Paul created his own religion, one in which he would play a prominent role. According to Hyam Maccoby, in his book, *The Mythmaker*:

> Paul was the greatest fantasist of all. He created the Christian myth by deifying Jesus, a Jewish Messiah figure whose real aims were on the plane of Jewish political Utopianism. Paul transformed Jesus' death into a cosmic sacrifice in which the powers of evil sought to overwhelm the power of good... The myth adumbrated by Paul was then brought into full imaginative life in the Gospels, which were written under the influence of Paul's ideas and for the use of the Pauline Christian Church.[152]

---

150 Michael Martin, *The Case Against Christianity* (Philadelphia, Temple University Press, 1991) p. 59
151 Charles Guignebert, *Jesus* Trans. S. H. Hooke (New Hyde Park, New York: University Book, 1956) p. 66
152 Hyam Maccoby, *The Mythmaker: Paul and the Invention of Christianity*

Another version is that Jesus was simply a good teacher. After His death, the word of Jesus' teachings began to spread. As these accounts spread, they became embellished with stories of miracles to give them more credibility and authority. The person of Jesus took on mythological proportions that caused the stories of His miracles to become even grander.

The view of Jesus as simply a good teacher is essentially the position of many liberal theologians. As such, much of the push in liberal theology looks beyond the New Testament to discover the "true" Jesus.

We can see such an approach in John Dominic Crossan's books *Jesus: A Revolutionary Biography* and *The Historical Jesus: The Life of a Mediterranean Jewish Peasant*. According to Crossan, Jesus was a "peasant Jewish Cynic."[153]

This is also why the Jesus Seminar sought to determine which sayings of Jesus in the Bible are authentic. After all, why try to determine the true sayings of Jesus unless you believe that some of his statements in the New Testament are false?

On the other extreme is the belief that Jesus was something of a con artist. This view is perhaps the oldest of all and has been put forth again in a book by the historian Morton Smith, *Jesus The Magician*.[154]

Smith writes that Jesus went to Egypt as a young man, possibly to look for work. While in Egypt, He began to study the art of magic. When Jesus returned to Judea, He began to work "miracles" using His new skills.

Jesus' skill as a magician began to attract large crowds. As the crowds started to build, so did the opposition. After His death, in an attempt to refute the charges against Jesus, the disciples removed the magical elements from the Gospel accounts.

(New York: Harper & Row, 1986) pp. 204&5

153 John Dominic Crossan, *Jesus: A Revolutionary Biography* (San Francisco, Harper, 1995) p. 198

154 Morton Smith, *Jesus the Magician* (San Francisco: Harper & Row, 1978)

While most critics accept one or more of these theories, what is the evidence for them? As shown in the first book in this series, the Gospels present a reliable picture of events. Admittedly, however, this is only one side of the story. Other early references to Jesus are neither Christian nor friendly.

Early Non-Christian References

The Jewish historian Josephus has the earliest references to Jesus by a non-Christian writer. In his book *Antiquities of the Jews*, which he finished in the year A.D. 93 or 94, Josephus refers to Jesus twice.

The first reference is also one of the most disputed passages concerning Jesus, for it seems to have been altered at some time by Christians. The first passage, as we now have it, states:

> Now, there was about this time Jesus, a wise man, if it be lawful to call him a man, for he was a doer of wonderful works - a teacher of such men as receive the truth with pleasure. He drew over to him both many of the Jews and many of the Gentiles. He was [the] Christ; and when Pilate, at the suggestion of the principal men amongst us, had condemned him to the cross, those that loved him at the first did not forsake him, for he appeared to them alive again the third day, as the divine prophets had foretold these and ten thousand other wonderful things concerning him; and the tribe of Christians, so named from him, are not extinct at this day.[155]

Many scholars have pointed out that for Josephus to have written such an account, he would have been a Christian. An orthodox Jew would not have written things like "if it be lawful to call him a man" and "He was [the] Christ."

Since there is no indication that Josephus was a Christian, it would seem clear that someone altered the passage. The real question is: Did Josephus write any of it, or is the entire passage a forgery?

Research on a recently discovered Arabic manuscript of Josephus supports the notion that he is responsible for most of the

---

155 Josephus, *Antiquities of the Jews*, XVIII.III.3

passage. Schlomo Pines, a professor at Hebrew University in Jerusalem, found that the Arabic version did not contain the questionable phrases. The Arabic version reads as follows:

> At this time there was a wise man who was called Jesus. And his conduct was good and (he) was known to be virtuous. And many people from among the Jews and other nations became his disciples. Pilate condemned him to be crucified and to die. And those who had become his disciples did not abandon his discipleship. They reported that he had appeared to them three days after his crucifixion and that he was alive; accordingly he was perhaps the messiah concerning whom the prophets have recounted wonders.[156]

In this version, Josephus does not say that Jesus is the Christ, but only that "perhaps" He was. He does not say Christ had risen from the dead, only that His disciples "reported" that they had seen Jesus. There is nothing in this passage that Josephus could not have written.

The only other passage in which Josephus mentions Jesus refers to Him as simply the brother of James.

> Festus was now dead, and Albinus was but upon the road; so he assembled the Sanhedrim of judges, and brought before them the brother of Jesus, who was called Christ, whose name was James.[157]

This passage does not call Jesus the Christ. In fact, the way Josephus refers to Jesus here as the so-called Christ is derogatory. Thus, just as most scholars believe a Jew could not have written the first passage, they do not believe a Christian could have written this passage. Therefore, scholars accept the second passage as authentic.

In the second passage, Josephus mentions Jesus as a way of identifying Jesus' brother, James, to the reader. This use implies that Josephus had already introduced Jesus.

---

156 Quoted by Gary R Habermas, *The Verdict of History* (Nashville, Tennessee: Thomas Nelson, 1988) pp. 91-92
157 Josephus, *Antiquities of the Jews* XX.IX.I

Because of this, and that it is unlikely that Christians would have been able to alter the Arabic version of Josephus, most scholars now accept that Christians did not add the first passage but altered it.

These two passages provide a non-Christian witness to the fact that Jesus did at least exist and the significant events recorded in the Gospels, the Romans crucified him during the rule by Pilate and his disciples' report of having seen him risen three days later is correct.

The Jewish Talmud, compiled near the end of the first century and during the second, also mentions Jesus. In one passage, it reads,

> On the eve of the Passover Yeshu was hanged. For forty days before the execution took place, a herald went forth and cried, "He is going forth to be stoned because he has practiced sorcery and enticed Israel to apostasy. Any one who can say anything in his favour, let him come forward and plead on his behalf." But since nothing was brought forward in his favour he was hanged on the eve of the Passover.[158]

The word for *hanged* used here sometimes refers to someone who hung on a cross. From this passage, we learn that Jesus (Yeshu) was a religious leader who practiced what the Jews called sorcery. His followers would call them miracles. We see that Jesus had a large following, for he "enticed Israel to apostasy," and his crucifixion occurred on the eve of the Passover.

Other references in Jewish writings reflect on Christian teachings. For example, we can see that some Jews needed to respond to the virgin birth stories because Jewish writings sometimes refer to Jesus as "Jesus son of Pandera." Pandera was supposedly a Roman soldier.[159]

The Roman historian Thallus, who wrote a history of the world around A.D. 52, seems to have included a discussion of the events concerning Jesus' death in his history. While we do not have Thal-

---

158 Quoted in Habermas, *The Verdict* p. 98
159 Craig Blomberg, *The Historical Reliability of the Gospels* (Dowers Grove, Ill: Inter-Varsity, 1987) pp. 198-9

lus's writings, we know of the existence of this history because other writers from that period refer to it.

One of the works that mentioned Thallus is by the early Christian historian Julius Africanus. While discussing the death of Jesus and the darkness that preceded it, Julius Africanus wrote the following:

> Thallus, in the third book of his history, calls this darkness an eclipse of the sun, but in my opinion he is wrong.[160]

The debate concerning Christ and the events surrounding his death seemed to be in progress by the middle of the first century.

Cornelius Tacitus, one of the greatest Roman historians, also mentioned Christ in his *Annals,* written about A.D. 110. During his description of the burning of Rome, Tacitus wrote that rumors were spreading that Nero had set the fire himself. Tacitus wrote of Nero,

> Consequently, to get rid of the report, Nero fastened the guilt and inflicted the most exquisite tortures on a class hated for their abominations, called Christians by the populace. Christus, from whom the name had its origin, suffered the extreme penalty during the reign of Tiberius at the hands of one of our procurators, Pontius Pilate, and a deadly superstition, thus checked for the moment, again broke out not only in Judaea, the first source of the evil, but also in the City [Rome], where all things hideous and shameful from every part of the world meet and become popular.[161]

We see that Christianity had spread only a short time after Jesus's death and had encountered significant opposition.

What does it all Mean?

What do these non-Christian sources reveal about Jesus? Most important is what they do not say, as these writers did not agree with what the Christians were saying about Christ.

---

160 Quoted in *Habermas,* The Verdict p. 93
161 Tactius, *Annals* 15:44 quoted in Paul Barnett, *Is the New Testament History?* (Ann Arbor, MI: Vine Books, 1986) p. 20

Tacitus called Christianity a "deadly superstition" and "hideous." We expect these authors to make the strongest arguments against Jesus and Christianity possible. If Jesus had only been a creation of Paul, who did not exist, would not at least one of these early critics have pointed this out?

Some argued that these writers lived too long after the events to know what had happened. This argument ignores that the controversy concerning Jesus did not begin during the second century. As shown by these critics, it started much earlier.

The opposition to Jesus started while He was still alive. It is seen in the Gospels and in the earliest letters of Paul, which even liberal scholars accept as written around the middle of the first century. The early opponents of Christianity would have known of the events that surrounded the life of Jesus. Still, the opponents of Christianity who were alive during the time of Christ or lived close enough to the events to have talked to those who did never argued that Jesus did not exist.

What we see with many of these non-Christian sources is an acceptance of the claims of Christianity, with attempts to provide alternative explanations. Take, for example, the Virgin Birth.

The Talmud does not dispute the biblical claim that Joseph was not Jesus' natural father. Instead, the Talmud writers claim the only natural explanation: that another man was Jesus' father.

More specifically, they argue that Jesus' father had been a Roman soldier named Pandera. Christian scholars have long pointed out the similarity of this name to the Greek word *Parthenos* (virgin). They have concluded that the name chosen for Jesus' father is simply a derogatory corruption of the Greek word for virgin.

Interestingly, making Jesus' father a Roman soldier would also preclude another claim that Christ made: that he was a descendant of King David.

As for the miracles recorded in the Gospels, those who lived at the time of Jesus' ministry or shortly after that did not attempt to claim that they never occurred. Instead, they tried to explain them away.

Jesus claimed that the miracles were a sign from God to prove that He was the Son of God. The Talmud, however, does not refer to miracles done by the power of God but to "*sorcery,*" the acts of a magician.

Implicit in this explanation is that some miraculously appearing events did occur. They disputed the reason for these events but not their occurrence.

We can see this tacit acceptance of Christian claims in Thallus' explanation for the sun's darkening just before Jesus's death. Thallus accepted that there was a period of darkness when Jesus died.

Rather than trying to dispute the darkness, he attempted to provide a natural explanation, which did not require Jesus to be who He claimed. As such, Thallus offers evidence to support the biblical claims for darkness at the time of Christ's death, even if he questioned the cause of that darkness.

Since Jesus' crucifixion happened during the Passover, and the Passover occurs during the full moon, we know that an eclipse could not have caused this darkness. Eclipses occur during a new moon.[162]

From the writings of the early critics, we learn that there was a religious teacher named Jesus. They tell us that His birth was unusual. During His ministry, Jesus did many things that seemed miraculous.

He had a large following, and the religious leaders of the time opposed Him. We learn that Jesus was arrested while in Jerusalem for the Passover. He was condemned to death by the Roman governor Pontius Pilate. His death was by crucifixion.

---

162 A full moon occurs when the earth is between the moon and the sun. A new moon is when the moon is between the earth and the sun. If during a new moon, the moon moves directly in front of the sun, you have an eclipse. Since an eclipse can occur only during a new moon and the Passover occurs during a full moon, the darkness could not have been caused by an eclipse.

During the crucifixion, there was an unexplained darkening of the sky. Finally, His followers claimed that Jesus rose from the dead three days later and still lives.

Admittedly, this is not proof that Jesus is the Son of God. However, we must remember that this evidence is from the early critics of Christianity, who are not usually considered a rich source of supporting material. We can assume that these critics used what they thought to be the strongest arguments against Christianity. As such, they indirectly tell us what these writers did not consider a good argument.

Putting It All Together

How does this evidence help answer the question posed at the beginning of this chapter: Who is Jesus? We can reject the claim that Jesus did not exist. If those closest to the events accepted Jesus as a historical person, it would be challenging two thousand years later to make a strong case that He wasn't.

The theory that the historical Jesus, while an actual person, bears little resemblance to the Jesus of the Bible is also questionable. The difficulty is that the only sources we have for learning about the historical Jesus are the books of the New Testament, the writings of early Christians, and the writings of early critics.

Not even the early critics dispute the main points of the Gospel accounts. Instead, they try to provide alternative explanations for them. Thus, the supporters of this theory must try to argue that the historical Jesus was different than the only accounts we have of him. The question is: On what basis do they reject the Jesus portrayed in the New Testament?

While the belief that Jesus was a magician has some support among the early critics, it also contains some fatal flaws. The argument for this position can be summarized as follows:

> A. Jesus appeared to do miracles.
> B. Miracles cannot happen.
> C. The Gospels reveal parallels between the actions of Jesus and ancient magical practices.
> Therefore: Jesus must have been a magician.

While Christians would agree with premise A, they would question B and C, and thus the conclusion. For one thing, while the Gospels date from the first century, the sources of information we have on ancient magical practices come hundreds of years later.

This immediately raises the question of who influenced whom. Those supporting the magician theory are in the awkward position of trying to claim that the later sources influenced the earlier ones.

There is also the problem of the parallels themselves. The parallels rest primarily on the claim that many of Jesus' miracles look like things attributed to magicians of the time.

The Gospels report that Jesus cast out demons, a claim commonly made by magicians. One problem with claiming this as a parallel is that the Gospels portray the miracles of Jesus as divine acts, not the acts of a magician (Acts 2:22).

In his book, *Jesus the Magician*, Smith acknowledges this problem. Still, he claims that the early Christian writers sanitized the miracles' stories to remove all magical elements. While claiming that early Christians removed the magical elements may solve the problem, no evidence supports this contention.

Another problem is that not all of the miracles have such magical parallels. The feeding of the five thousand has no parallel in ancient magical practice. This miracle does not fit the picture of Jesus as a magician, thereby supporting His claim to be God.

How does Smith fit these miracles into his theory? Smith puts them into the following category,

> control of purely physical objects. Since these miracles are the most clearly impossible, stories about them are the most surely false and among the most likely to be secondary developments of the tradition.[163]

Smith deals with the miracles that do not fit his theory by writing them off as later, unhistorical additions. It is no wonder that Smith can find support for his theory in the Gospels since anything

163 Smith, *Jesus* p. 118

that should be there yet isn't he writes off as the result of sanitizing the Gospels. Anything that shouldn't be there is, he claims are later additions. If you adjust the evidence enough, any theory can fit.

Miracles

The key to the theory that Jesus was a magician is the belief that miracles cannot happen. We can see this belief when Smith attempts to provide "magical" explanations for the miracles recorded in the Gospels. Smith writes:

> Most of the miracles reported are possible, if stripped of the "explanations" that make them miracles. For example: Jesus could not cast out demons; there are none. But he could and probably did quiet lunatics, and the reports of "casting out demons" are merely reports of quieting lunatics (what observably happened) with built-in demonological "explanations."[164]

This rejection of the supernatural is at the heart of most rejections of the traditional accounts of Jesus. Critics ground these rejections not on facts but on an underlying philosophy of secularism.

When the Gospels speak of Jesus as God incarnate who did miracles, healed the sick, cured the blind, and rose from the dead, from the viewpoint of secularism, the Gospels must be wrong. These sorts of things just do not happen.

The secularist writes off the Gospel accounts of miracles as either the work of a magician or as the creations of later writers trying to give Jesus more credibility.

When they cannot simply write off a miracle, they rationalize them away. As the historian Michael Grant wrote concerning the miracle of the feeding of the five thousand:

What, in fact, did Jesus do? We cannot say for certain. But we can, on this particular occasion, rationalize. Rationalization, the foisting of materialistic interpretations upon the miracles, is a familiar process which has been with us for hundreds of years. It is

---

164 Smith, *Jesus* p. 149

not always very profitable. But in this case it is legitimate because Jesus must have done *something*.[165]

The possibility that Jesus may have actually done the miracle does not seem to have occurred to Grant. That Jesus might have fed five thousand people with only five loaves of bread and two fish is not even considered. Why? For Grant, miracles cannot happen, so there must be another explanation.

Some have even tried to show that miracles can't occur. The eighteenth-century Scottish philosopher David Hume put forth the most famous of these arguments. According to Hume:

> A miracle is a violation of the laws of nature; and as a firm and unalterable experience has established these laws, the proof against a miracle, from the very nature of the fact, is as entire as any argument from experience can possibly be imagined… Nothing is esteemed a miracle if it ever happens in the common course of nature… There must be an experience against every miraculous event, otherwise the event would not merit that appellation.[166]

In other words, Hume says that a miracle is, by definition, an event that cannot happen. Since miracles cannot occur, they have not happened. Anything that does happen, however improbable, cannot be considered a miracle but must instead be a natural event.

Hume's basis for this conclusion is the belief that the laws of nature prohibit miracles. One problem with this view is that Hume based it on a Newtonian view of the universe, where everything is a matter of fixed mathematics. But in quantum physics, things are not quite so fixed; instead, they are issues of probability.

A deeper problem is Hume's observation that natural laws are grounded in "a firm and unalterable experience." Miracles cannot happen because human experience tells us that the laws of nature have never been broken. Since miracles have not happened, they cannot occur.

165 Michael Grant, *Jesus: An Historian's Review of the Gospel* (New York: Charles Scribner's Sons, 1977) p. 42
166 David Hume, *An Enquiry Concerning Human Understanding* (Chicago: Open court, 1958) pp. 126-7

But do we truly have such an unalterable experience? What about the thousands of reports of miracles recorded not only in the Bible but throughout human history?

While many of these miracles might have natural explanations, can we confidently say this about every single one? No. We have already seen this to be the case with some of Jesus' miracles.

While some critics admit that something occurred, they can't say what. They cannot rule out a supernatural explanation. The only way the critics could be sure that miracles have not occurred is if they proclaim that miracles cannot happen.

Yet, this results in the fallacy of circular reasoning, as the reason given that miracles cannot occur is that they have not occurred. Hume argues that miracles are impossible because they have never happened. We know miracles have never occurred because they are impossible, and we know that they are impossible because they have never occurred and...

Even though Hume's argument against miracles is logically flawed, his conclusion that miracles are impossible still forms the basis for much of the "modern" thought concerning the Bible. As we have seen, if we reject miracles, we must reject the biblical accounts that record them.

For many, this rejection of the supernatural has defined the modern approach to the Bible. Guignebert wrote concerning this,

> Ever since investigators, unbiased by religious motives, first applied themselves to the study of the problem of Christianity, not one has failed to reach the fundamental conclusion that the traditional explanation, the orthodox account of Christian origins, will not bear critical examination.[167]

While this may initially seem a powerful indictment against Christianity, upon closer examination, it reveals the problem with much of modern scholarship. Guignebert does not say that all investigators have concluded that the traditional explanation for

---

167 Guignebert, Jesus, p. 1

Christianity's origin, the one recorded in the Bible, is false. He says that only those "unbiased by religious motives" have.

In effect, Guignebert says you are unbiased if you agree with him. If, on the other hand, you conclude that the biblical record is correct, then you must have been influenced by religious beliefs.

This attitude reveals the tremendous bias against traditional religion in much of modern scholarship. How could anyone accept the "traditional explanation," the explanation that says Jesus is God incarnate, that He did many miracles, that He died on the cross for the sins of the world, that He was resurrected and appeared to many people, and that from this came the Christian church, and not fall under Guignebert's classification as biased?

Which is the unbiased position, the one that rejects all miraculous events no matter what or believes miracles are possible and considers the evidence for them on a case-by-case basis?

John Dominic Crossan also rejects those who defend the Biblical accounts as accurate out of hand. In describing his approach, he states that giving,

> an accurate but impartial account of the historical Jesus as distinct from the confessional Christ... is what the academic or scholarly study of the historical Jesus is about, at least when it is not for doing theology and calling it history, doing autobiography and calling it biography, doing Christian apologetics and calling it academic scholarship.[168]

Like Guignebert, Crossan also seems to assume that the only impartial researchers are those who end up rejecting the "confessional Christ" as historically valid.

While his statement may seem valid at first glance, closer examination again reveals a strong bias. For example, he rejects the idea that Christian apologetics can be considered scholarship. Christian apologetics is simply the study of the evidence in favor of Christianity. As such, skeptics often criticize apologetics, as Crossan does here, as not being scholarship since it aims to defend Christianity.

168 Crossan, *Jesus*, p xi

There are two problems with such criticism. First and most important is that all people are apologists for their positions; liberal scholars are no different. Is Crossan really trying to say that his books are not defending the positions he holds?

This myth of neutrality probably explains why most liberal theologians rarely, if ever, seriously deal with conservative scholars and their arguments. They reject traditional arguments out of hand as biased and thus unworthy of consideration.

As a result, they start with an a priori rejection of the supernatural under the guise of being scientific. Then, they insulate themselves from conflicting points of view on the pretext of objectivity.

The second problem is that Crossan assumes that the conclusions reached by Christian apologists are reached only because of bias, not because of evidence. In other words, they are Christians, so they reach Christian conclusions.

This argument commits the logical fallacy of *Poisoning the Well*, one of the five forms of *ad hominem* attack or attacking the person instead of the argument. While individual Christians may be biased, this argument again assumes that Christianity is false. This assumption can be seen in Crossan's distinction between the Jesus of history and the Jesus of faith as if they could not be the same.

Thus, while it is possible that a Christian apologist reaches the particular conclusions they hold because they are Christians, it is also possible that they are a Christian because the evidence led them to these conclusions.[169]

Michael Martin takes a slightly different approach to the miracles of Jesus, for Martin does not rule out the possibility of miracles. Instead, he says that they are virtually impossible to prove.

For example, Martin suggests that Jesus' miracles may have been due to "unknown scientific laws," "deception, fraud,

---

169 As it turns out this happens to be the case with this author. I did not grow up as a Christian, and in fact was for a time an atheist. I became a Christian as a result of examining the evidence.

or trickery," or simply "rare occurrences of uncaused events."[170] Therefore, even if the evidence supports that the "miracles" occurred, this is not enough for Martin.

The main problem with Martin's position is that the evidence does not support it; instead, it is an attempt to avoid the conclusion to which the evidence points. As such, it reveals Martin's bias against the supernatural.

Does the evidence support the notion that Jesus was a swindler? Are we really to believe that Jesus had access to scientific knowledge that still remains unknown 2000 years later? Is it reasonable to think that Jesus could call upon "rare occurrences of uncaused events" seemingly at will?

Conclusion

The historical record is clear. Nearly 2000 years ago, there lived a man whose ministry lasted only three and a half years. He died alone, and almost all his friends and family deserted him. He could not afford a grave, left no writings, and seemed destined to disappear, not even making so much as a footnote in history.

And yet, in terms of the impact on the course of history and the lives He has affected, Jesus Christ is the most important person ever. The religion He founded has become the largest in the world.[171]

Not only do critics' explanations fail to explain who Jesus is, but they also fail to explain the phenomena of Christianity. How did the life of a single man grow to become the most important factor in shaping world history?

As an example of how remarkable this truly is, let us examine the life of a man who lived a short time after Jesus. His name was

---

170 Martin, *Case*, pp. 151-3

171 As of 1988, Christianity had 1,644,396,500 followers or about 32.9 percent of the world's population. The next largest religion is Islam with 860,388,300 - about 17.2 percent of the world's population. (*The World Almanac And Book Of Facts - 1989*, p. 591)

ben Kosiba. While his name may not be familiar to most people, ben Kosiba greatly impacted the Jewish nation.

In A.D. 132, ben Kosiba began and led the final Jewish revolt against the Roman Empire. The rebellion lasted for three years. Ben Kosiba ruled Israel during that time, and many Jews proclaimed him the Messiah.

The Romans finally quelled the rebellion and beheaded ben Kosiba, but only after 500,000 Jews had been killed and nearly a thousand villages completely destroyed.[172]

Both Jesus' ministry and ben Kosiba's revolt lasted about three years. Both were proclaimed to be the Messiah, and the Romans executed both. Jesus had only a small group of followers at the time of His death. In contrast, ben Kosiba probably had the support of over a million people.

Despite this, ben Kosiba disappeared into historical obscurity, so much so that until 1951, we did not even know his name. Jesus went on to become one of the most well-known figures in all of history. What was it about Jesus that led to this growth and expansion of the religion that He founded?

From the Christian point of view, this is precisely what one would expect. If God truly did take on a human body and live among His creations, we would expect Him to have had such an impact – to literally change the course of history.

Can any of the theories put forth by the critics shed any light on this? Who is Jesus Christ? The only real answer to this question posed by Jesus near Caesarea Philippi remains the one that Peter gave:

"You are the Christ, the Son of the living God."
(Matthew 16:15)

---

172 Barnett, *Is the New*, p. 9

6

Resurrection Or Passover Plot?

The resurrection of Jesus Christ is one of the most wicked, vicious, heartless hoaxes ever foisted upon the minds of men, or it is the most fantastic fact of history.
(Josh McDowell)[173]

AFTER THE DEATH of Jesus, many who had opposed His ministry were determined to see that it died with Him. Few were as committed to this goal as Saul of Tarsus. Saul was a man of action, and it was not his way to sit on the sidelines and hope that someone would stop this new movement.

Shortly after the stoning of Stephen, the church's first martyr, he began to arrest Christians. Saul soon came to be hated and feared by the fledgling church in Jerusalem. Because of this persecution, the church in Jerusalem was broken up and forced to flee. Eventually, Jerusalem had few active Christians.

While the persecution severely limited the church's activities in Jerusalem, it had some positive effects. As Christians left to avoid arrest, they took their faith with them, scattering it throughout the countryside.

One of the cities that developed a strong church was Damascus. As a major trading center with a large Jewish population, Damascus could be critical for spreading Christianity.

---

173 Josh McDowell, *Evidence That Demands a Verdict,* (San Bernardino, CA: Here's Life, 1979) p 179

Realizing this, Saul went to the Sanhedrin for authority to arrest Christians there. Having received the authority, Saul set out. But the fervent persecutor of Christians never arrived. On the way to Damascus, something happened that literally changed Saul's life forever.

During that trip, Saul became the man better known to us by his Roman name, Paul,[174] the Apostle to the Gentiles. What happened? How did a man who had devoted his life to eradicating Christianity suddenly turn around 180 degrees and dedicate his life to spreading the Gospel? The answer is simple: Saul encountered the resurrected Christ.

Critics of Christianity recognize that the resurrection is central to the Christian faith. Charles Guignebert wrote concerning the resurrection that "there would have been no Christianity if the belief in the resurrection had not been founded and systematized."[175]

Christians consider the resurrection to be more than just a significant historical development. It is essential to the Faith. The apostle Paul wrote to the Christians in the city of Corinth,

> For what I received I passed on to you as of first importance: that Christ died for our sins according to the Scriptures, that he was buried, that he was raised on the third day according to the Scriptures ... and if Christ has not been raised, our preaching is useless and so is your faith. (1 Corinthians 15:3-4 & 14)

So what happened that first Easter morning? What happened to bring about the change in Paul from persecutor to defender of the faith? What transformed Peter from the man who would not even admit to a servant girl that he knew Jesus into the man who forcefully proclaimed Jesus to a massive crowd on Pentecost?

---

174 As a citizen of Rome and a Jew, Paul would have been given both names at birth.

175 Charles Guignebert, *Jesus* Trans. S. H. Hooke (New Hyde Park, New York: University Books, 1956) p. 536

Only a short time after he denied Jesus, Peter stood before the Sanhedrin and said,

> Judge for yourselves whether it is right in God's sight to obey you rather than God. For we cannot help speaking about what we have seen and heard. (Acts 4:19-20)

Because of the dramatic changes in the disciples' lives and the boldness of their subsequent actions, most critics accept that something happened that first Easter morning. Guignebert writes concerning the resurrection,

> There is not the shadow of a doubt that the disciples believed in the reality of the appearances, nor can we deny that they possessed some kind of reality, but it remains to discover what kind of reality."[176]

In his book *Who was Jesus*, Colin Cross wrote, "All that can be stated for certain about the resurrection is that a small group of people really believed it happened."[177]

Because of the central role of the resurrection and its importance to Christianity, many critics worked hard to disprove it. Over the years, critics have put forth several theories attempting to provide a credible explanation for the events of that first Easter morning.

As their starting point, most critics, directly or indirectly, attempt to discredit the biblical accounts. Usually, this is done by citing the supposed conflicting nature of the various Gospel accounts.

Cross writes concerning the biblical accounts of the resurrection that "it is impossible to get to the bottom of the story. The accounts in the Gospels are different and inconsistent."[178] In his book *Jesus: The Evidence*, Ian Wilson wrote: "The various accounts of the scene at the empty tomb on the first Easter morning are so full of inconsistencies that it is easy to deride them."[179]

176 Guignebert, *Jesus*, p. 517

177 Colin Cross, *Who Was Jesus* (New York: Atheneum, 1970) p. 111

178 Cross, *Who*, p. 109

179 Ian Wilson, *Jesus: the Evidence* (San Francisco: Harper & Row, 1984) p.

Michael Martin, in his book *The Case Against Christianity*, claims that,

> In sum, the accounts of what happened at the tomb are ei-
> ther inconsistent or can only be made consistent with the aid
> of implausible interpretations. Without such interpretations
> they simply could not all be true. The accounts of what hap-
> pens in the days after finding the empty tomb, although not
> perhaps contradictory, are certainly very different and hard to
> reconcile.[180]

So before we begin to examine the different theories put forth by the critics, let us review the Gospel accounts of Jesus' death and resurrection to see if we can dismiss them as quickly as the critics suggest.

Jesus is Arrested

Time: Late Thursday night or early Friday morning.
Matthew 26:47-56   Mark 14:43-52
Luke 22:47-53   John 18:1-11

It was the week of the Passover, the time when Jews commemo-rate their deliverance from Egypt, and Jesus had come to Jerusalem. The previous Sunday, He had been welcomed as the King, for many believed He was the Messiah who would overthrow Roman rule.

During the week, tensions between Jesus and the temple priests grew. On Thursday, Jesus and his disciples ate the Passover meal in the city: a meal that has come to be known as the Last Supper. Later, they crossed the valley east of Jerusalem and went to the Mount of Olives. There, in the Garden of Gethsemane, Jesus spent the night in prayer.

All four Gospels record that sometime during the night, Ju-das led a group sent by the chief priests to arrest Jesus. Judas had

---

180 Michael Martin, *The Case Against Christianity* (Philadelphia: Temple University Press, 1991) p. 81

planned to betray Jesus with a kiss, and John's Gospel records their conversation.

When the disciples realized what was happening, some tried to prevent the arrest. One of those with Jesus cut off the ear of a servant of the high priest. John tells us that it was Peter.

Jesus stopped His disciples and then let the guards lead Him away. Mark alone includes an account of a young man who tried to follow Jesus but was chased off. The way Mark writes this leads some to conclude that the young man was Mark himself.

Before the Sanhedrin

> Time: Early Friday morning to Sunrise.
> Matthew 26:57-68, 27:1   Mark 14:53-65, 15:1
> Luke 22:47-53, 63-71   John 18:12-14, 19-24

After the arrest, John records that the guards took Jesus to Annas's house for questioning. Before the Romans removed him, Annas had been the high priest, and many still considered him the real one. Annas questioned Jesus before sending Him to the current high priest, Caiaphas, for a formal trial before the Sanhedrin.

The Sanhedrin was the highest legal authority for the Jews and functioned as a sort of supreme court in matters of religion. Both Matthew and Mark record the details of the trial.

After the trial, they blindfolded and beat Jesus. The guards mocked Him by asking Jesus to prophesy which one of them had just hit Him. Just after sunrise, the Sanhedrin met once again to formalize their decision to put Jesus to death.

Peter's Denial of Jesus

> Time: Early Friday morning before Sunrise.
> Matthew 26:69-74   Mark 14:66-72
> Luke 22:54-62   John 18:15-18

All four Gospels record the denial of Peter. The Gospels of Matthew and Mark mention it after Jesus's trial. Luke, who does not include the trial's details, mentions it between his account of Jesus at the High Priest's house and the guards beating him. John interweaves Peter's denial with his description of the trial. It would seem that Peter's denial of Jesus occurred simultaneously with the trial before the Sanhedrin.

Peter had followed Jesus from the garden. When they took Jesus in for trial, Peter remained outside in the courtyard and began to warm himself by the fire. Three times, those around him asked him if he was a disciple of Jesus, and three times he denied that he knew Jesus.

Just after the third denial, the rooster began to crow. Suddenly, Peter remembers the words that Jesus had spoken just a few hours before, "this very night, before the rooster crows, you will disown me three times" (Matthew 26:34).

There are two differences in these accounts that critics cite as contradictions. The first, while Mark mentions that the rooster crowed twice, the other three Gospels only say that the rooster crowed.

This is hardly a contradiction. None of the four accounts present a complete picture with all the details of the three denials. The Gospel writers chose one of the three denials and briefly mentioned the others.

Each writer left out some details in their account. The fact that the three writers did not mention that the rooster crowed twice does not make them wrong or mean their accounts contradict the one that did.

Another consideration is that we all have our own perspective of events. If a group of people all see the same event and then compare their 'eyewitness' testimony, there will be differences.

While it is true that some of these differences might be the result of errors, that is not the only reason. The accounts could all be correct, as I believe the Biblical accounts are, and still differ in some details.

These differences are because, with any given event, we cannot notice many things going on. When people watch a movie for the second time, they often see something they did not notice the first time.

As such, one possible reason for some of the minor differences in the gospel accounts may be that different people noticed different aspects of the events they witnessed.

One person may have noticed the number of times the rooster crowed, while the others only noted that the rooster crowed. It does not necessarily mean either is wrong; it may only mean they noticed different things.

There is also the issue that it is clear some gospel writers knew of others. As a result, when they wrote their Gospels, they may have given some details only summarized by the earlier Gospel.

I believe this explains why John is so different from the other three Gospels. John seems intent on adding perspective and details not mentioned by the others. This explanation fits well with John's closing statement,

There are many other things that Jesus did. If every one of them were written down, I suppose the whole world would not have room for the books that would be written. (John 21:25)

These differences are not a reason to call the accounts into question. Instead, it is yet more evidence for the reliability of the text, as it is the nature of actual eyewitness testimony to contain such minor differences.

If the accounts agreed even on such minor details, it would indicate some artificial collusion. You can tell that a group of people are lying if their stories agree too much, for this shows some agreed-upon story instead of actual recollections of what happened.

The other alleged contradiction is that in the Gospels of Matthew and Mark, Peter makes his second denial to a woman, while in Luke and John, it is to a man. Looking at these four passages carefully, we see that the woman does not address her charges directly to Peter in Matthew and Mark. Instead, she tells them to a crowd that had gathered.

Both Matthew and Mark have Peter responding to these charges. There are two possibilities. The first is that Peter overheard the women's charges and responded to the woman directly. However, this would seem odd as the accounts portray him as trying to avoid confrontation.

Another possibility is someone in the crowd approached Peter to ask him about the charges. From the accounts in Luke and John, it seems the latter is what happened. As stated by Matthew and Mark, a woman was responsible for making the accusation. Still, they were presented to Peter by a man, as described in Luke and John.

Jesus Before Pilate and Herod

> Time: After Sunrise Friday morning.
> Matthew 27:2-26   Mark 15:1-15
> Luke 23:1-25   John 18:28-19:16

After the Sanhedrin had passed formal judgment, they took Jesus to the Roman governor, Pontius Pilate. The accounts recorded in the Gospels agree, except that Luke and John provide further details that the others do not mention.

The additional accounts are once again complementary rather than contradictory. Luke records that Jesus met with Pilate twice. Between these two meetings, Pilate sent Jesus to Herod the Tetrarch. While the other Gospel writers do not mention the meeting with Herod, they do not exclude the possibility.

Putting all four accounts together, the Jewish leaders took Jesus to Pilate. Since it was during the Passover, the Jewish leaders would not enter the palace, so Pilate came out to them. They told Pilate they wanted Jesus put to death for claiming to be the king of the Jews, but Roman law prohibited them from carrying out this sentence.

After questioning Jesus concerning the charges, Pilate told them he could find nothing that Jesus had done wrong. When the Jewish leaders mentioned Jesus had started in Galilee, Pilate saw a way to avoid dealing with the problem.

He sent Jesus to Herod, who had control over that region. Herod could not deal with him, for Jesus refused to speak. So Herod simply sent Him back to Pilate.

Pilate still looked for a way to avoid crucifixion. There was a custom of releasing one criminal requested by the people during the Passover. Pilate offered the people a choice between Jesus and Barabbas, a man accused of murder. The same people who had welcomed Jesus with praises one week earlier now chose Barabbas.

Pilate tried to please the people by having Jesus flogged. After the flogging, the Roman soldiers took a purple robe, the color of royalty, and put it on Jesus. They then made a crown of thorns and put it on his head. After this, they took turns slugging Him.

Pilate then led Jesus before the crowd for a second time, and the crowd cried out to crucify Him again. Pilate talked to Jesus one last time, and then, for a third time, Pilate brought Jesus before the crowd. For a third time, the crowd demanded that Jesus be crucified. At this point, Pilate agreed and turned Jesus over to the guards for crucifixion.

Crucifixion

> Time: About 9:00 A.M. Friday
> Matthew 27:32-44   Mark 15:21-32
> Luke 23:26-32   John 19:17-28

The Synoptic Gospels of Matthew, Mark, and Luke all record that after the beatings by the Roman guards, Jesus was too weak to carry His cross[181] more than a short distance. When He could bear

---

181 Those who were crucified only carried the crossbeam of the cross and not the entire cross.

it no further, the guards grabbed Simon of Cyrene from the crowd and forced him to carry the cross the rest of the way.

Luke tells us that a large multitude followed behind Jesus as He made his way to the place of crucifixion, which all Gospels give as Golgotha, literally the Skull. The main controversies with the crucifixion seem to be over the words on the sign nailed to the cross and the time of the crucifixion.

As detailed in volume one of this series, there is no discrepancy between Mark and John over the hour of the crucifixion. There are several ways we can reconcile these accounts, and the problem is the evidence is not clear enough to say which of the explanations is correct.

Still, critics have raised one other question concerning the passage in John. The Synoptic Gospels clearly state that Jesus was crucified on Friday. John says that Jesus was crucified "on the day of Preparation of Passover Week" (John 19:14), which has led some to conclude that John thought the crucifixion was on Thursday.

An understanding of the ancient Greek language clears up this inconsistency. When John wrote his Gospel during the first century, the Greek word for the day of preparation, *paraskeue* (Παρασκευή), was used synonymously with Friday. This meaning came about because every Friday is a day of preparation for the weekly Sabbath.[182] Thus, it is perfectly correct to translate the passage in John as "on Friday of Passover Week." Therefore, it agrees with the other Gospels.

The other issue deals with the wording of the sign nailed to the cross above Christ. While all four Gospels mention the sign, as seen in the following quotations, none have precisely the same wording.

Matthew	– THIS IS JESUS, KING OF THE JEWS
Mark	– THE KING OF THE JEWS
Luke	– THIS IS THE KING OF THE JEWS
John	– JESUS OF NAZARETH, THE KING OF THE JEWS

---

182 Gleason Archer, *Encyclopedia of Bible Difficulties* (Grand Rapids: Zondervan, 1982) pp. 375-6

While these differences may seem trivial for accounts that only summarize events, critics have cited them as a problem. There is a possible explanation that would account for these minor differences. John tells us that the sign had three languages: Aramaic, Latin, and Greek.

That these messages may not have been precisely the same in each of these languages is a possibility. The Gospel writers could have based their accounts of the sign on these different versions. In other words, one writer may have used the Greek version, while another may have used Latin. In any case, the differences are hardly enough to call the versions contradictory or questionable, even if they were all based on the same language.

Death and Burial

>   Time: Friday Noon to shortly after 6:00 P.M.
>   Matthew 27:45-66   Mark 15:33-47
>   Luke 23:44-56   John 19:28-42

Matthew, Mark, and Luke record that at approximately noon, darkness came over the countryside, which lasted until about 3:00 P.M. Matthew and Mark record that at about 3:00 P.M. Jesus cried out, "My God, My God, why have you forsaken me?"

Matthew, Mark, and John record that the Roman soldiers gave Jesus wine vinegar to drink,[183] and all four Gospels mention that Jesus cried out just before His death. Matthew, Mark, and Luke record many events that accompanied His death, such as the torn veil in the temple. All the Gospels point out that it was the women who stayed with Jesus to the end.

John tells us that some Jews were worried that the bodies might be left on the crosses during the Sabbath and consequently asked that the crucifixion be shortened. The soldiers broke the legs of the two criminals crucified with Jesus, but Jesus was already dead.

---

183 This was commonly done, not for humanitarian reasons, but to prevent death, and thus prolong the suffering.

Appearances, however, were not good enough. These soldiers were to kill three men, and they had better be dead. To make sure, one of the soldiers ran his spear through Jesus' side, resulting in "a sudden flow of blood and water." (John 19:34)

All the Gospels record that Joseph of Arimathea went to Pilate to ask for the body of Jesus. After being assured that Jesus was dead, Pilate granted the request.

It was approaching sunset, and there was very little time left before the beginning of the Sabbath. Joseph's own tomb was close by. So, with the help of Nicodemus, mentioned by John, he quickly wrapped up the body of Jesus and placed it in the tomb.

The women followed and watched the burial. They then went home to gather spices and perfumes so the body could be adequately prepared for burial after the Sabbath.

Matthew records that after the Sabbath began, the Jewish leaders went to Pilate again. This time, they wanted guards placed at the tomb to keep the disciples from stealing the body so they could claim Jesus had risen. It is unclear whether Pilate agreed to send a Roman Guard or allowed them to send their own Palace Guard. Still, Pilate did agree to seal the tomb and have guards posted.

Resurrection: The Visits to the Tomb

> Time: Saturday evening to Sunday morning.
> Matthew 28:1-15   Mark 16:1-11[184]
> Luke 24:1-12   John 20:1-18

Few biblical accounts raise more questions than the visits to the tomb on the first Easter morning. While mentioned in all four Gospels, many critics write off these accounts as entirely irreconcilable.

184 There is a textual problem with the last eleven verses (9-20) of Mark. These verses do not appear in some ancient manuscripts and some early church fathers questioned these verses. They are included here for sake of completeness. If these verses are not genuine, then questions concerning contradictions between them and the other Gospel accounts are moot.

Nothing could be further from the truth. Not only can the accounts be reconciled, but they are at least three different ways.[185] As such, the question is not whether we can reconcile them but which way is correct?

The first Easter morning was a time of great excitement, and many events happened quickly. The accounts in the Gospels are, by necessity, only summaries of these events. Most of the problems cited concern the number of women and angels involved.

Martin, for example, sees the following problems in the Gospel accounts of Mary's visits to the tomb:

> According to John, only Mary Magdalene came to the tomb when it was still dark, thus contradicting the three other Gospels... before she runs to tell Simon Peter and the disciples she does not see any angels, or a youth, thus contradicting the other three Gospels. Moreover, since there is no report of her entering the tomb before she tells Simon Peter and the disciples, Mark and Luke are contradicted.[186]

The four Gospels mention that the following women visited the tomb that morning:

Matthew: Mary Magdalene, "the other Mary"
Mark: Mary Magdalene, Mary the mother of James, Salome
Luke: Mary Magdalene, Mary the mother of James, Joanna, "the others"
John: Mary Magdalene

All four Gospels tell us that Mary Magdalene visited the tomb. If we assume that "the other Mary" of Matthew's Gospel is Mary, the mother of James, then she is mentioned in three Gospel accounts.

Luke says several women went to the tomb. The fact that John only mentions the most important person to visit the tomb does not exclude the possibility that others were with her.

185 D. A. Carson, *Matthew* in The Expositor's Bible Commentary ed. Frank E. Gaebelein (Grand Rapid, MI: Zondervan, 1984) p. 587
186 Martin, Case, p. 79

In fact, there is nothing that says Mary only went to the tomb once. As we will see shortly, likely, the visit recorded by John occurred later than the visit recorded in the other Gospels.

A similar argument applies to the number of angels. Matthew and Mark mention only one angel, while Luke mentions that there were two. There is a big difference between mentioning one angel and saying there was only one angel.

Matthew begins his account with the opening of the tomb. Early Sunday morning, as the women were on their way to the tomb, an angel descended from heaven, rolled away the stone, and rendered the guards unconscious.

Matthew then jumps ahead to the words the angel speaks to the women. Matthew does not say where the angels are, but when we read the accounts in Mark and Luke, we find that it was inside the tomb.

The women arrived and found the stone already rolled away. They entered and saw two angels who told them to go and tell the disciples what they had seen, which they did.

Luke and John tell us that after the women reported what they had seen, Simon Peter ran to the tomb to see what had happened. John mentions that he accompanied Peter. While in the tomb, they saw the burial cloth but no body. They then returned home.

Mary, who had either followed Peter and John or returned a short time later, remained at the tomb and began to cry. Looking inside, she once again saw the two angels.

Then Jesus came to her. At first, she did not recognize Him, but there was no doubt when He called her name. She ran to tell the disciples that she had seen Jesus, and he was alive!

A short time later, the other women returned to the tomb, most likely to look for Mary. They encountered the risen Jesus, who told them he would go to Galilee.

When the guards regained consciousness, they reported the empty tomb to the chief priest. Matthew records that they were paid to lie, spreading the story that the disciples had stolen the body.

Resurrection: Later Appearances

Time: The next 40 days.
Matthew 28:16-20   Mark 16:12-20[187]
Luke 24:13-53   John 20:19-21:25

The remaining accounts record a few of Jesus's many appearances over the next forty days. Luke tells us that the next appearance was to Cleopas, who tradition identifies as Jesus' uncle.

Cleopas and another man were on their way to the city of Emmaus when Jesus joined them and taught them the meaning of the resurrection. Afterward, both men returned to Jerusalem to tell the disciples what they had seen. The disciples told them that Simon Peter had also seen Jesus.

As the disciples were talking, Jesus appeared before them. At first the disciples thought that Jesus might have been a spirit or a ghost. But Jesus proved to them that he had risen from the grave by challenging them to "look at my hands and my feet. It is I myself! Touch me and see, a ghost does not have flesh and bones, as you see I have" (Luke 24:39).

Thomas was not present this time and refused to believe until he saw Jesus for himself. The following Sunday, Thomas got his chance when Jesus again appeared, this time before all the disciples.

The Gospels record that Jesus went to Galilee and visited the disciples by the sea and on a mountain. After forty days, Jesus went with his disciples to the Mount of Olives, a short distance from Jerusalem. After blessing them, He ascended into Heaven.

The accounts in the four Gospels are not contradictory. Each writer, as you might expect, summarizes the events surrounding the death and resurrection of Jesus differently. But none of the accounts excludes the others. While this is only one of three possible ways to harmonize these accounts, only one way is needed to show that the reports are not contradictory.

---

187 See previous note on page 151 .

Further Problems?

While the accounts are not contradictory, this is not the only way critics attack them. For example, Martin cites other reasons to reject the resurrection: those who reported the resurrection were unreliable, there were no eyewitnesses, and there is a lack of independent confirmation.

As for the reliability of the witnesses, critics based their claim on the general unreliability of the Bible. Yet, as detailed in volume one of this series, the evidence for the reliability of the Bible is strong.

As for the lack of eyewitnesses, Martin is only partially correct. There were indeed no eyewitnesses to the actual resurrection itself, but this proves little, and it is not clear that there would have been anything special to see.

For example, technically, there were eyewitnesses to the rising of Lazarus. Yet, all those present only witnessed him coming out of the tomb. More central to the issue is that there were eyewitnesses to Jesus' death and eyewitnesses who saw that Jesus was alive again three days after his death. This evidence is all that is needed to show a resurrection.

Concerning the lack of eyewitnesses, Martin claims,

> we have only one contemporary eyewitness account of a post resurrection appearance of Jesus, namely Paul's ... [and] we have no good reason to suppose that Paul's experience was not a hallucination.[188]

Martin bases this conclusion on liberal theories that reject Matthew's and John's authorship of the Gospels that bear their names. As detailed in Volume I, these theories are themselves suspect.

There are good reasons to believe that the Gospels of Matthew and John are accurate eyewitness accounts written by the Apostles.[189]

---

188 Martin, *Case*, p. 81-2
189 See D. A. Carson, Douglas Moo, Leon Morris, *An Introduction to the New Testament* (Grand Rapids, MI: Zondervan, 1992) Matthew: pp. 66-74; John: 138-157

In addition, there are good reasons to think that the Gospel of Mark derives directly from the teachings of Peter.[190]

Another problem for Martin is that, even if he is correct and Paul's is the only actual eyewitness account we have, it does not follow that Paul was the only eyewitness. In one of his earliest letters, Paul said in defense of the resurrection that Jesus "appeared to more than five hundred of the brothers at the same time, most of whom are still living" (1 Corinthians 15:6).

In other words, Paul was saying that those who did not believe him should go and ask those who saw it. For Paul, the resurrection was an empirical fact that could be tested and verified, and he challenged people to do so.

Martin's final point is that there were no independent confirmations of the resurrection. Martin bases much of this claim on his contention that we cannot even say that Jesus existed. As we saw in the last chapter, this does not hold up. Even early critics reported that the disciples said Jesus rose from the dead.

While it is true that no non-Christian source, as Martin puts it, "confirms the resurrection,"[191] could they reasonably be expected to do so? Is it reasonable to suppose that someone could believe that Jesus rose from the dead and yet not become a Christian?[192]

While some claim that the only people who saw Jesus were his followers, this is not wholly correct. As we saw at the beginning of this chapter, Paul was not a disciple of Jesus when he saw the risen Lord, but a severe critic and opponent.

---

190 Some scholars believe that the Gospel of Mark came from a series of Sermons given by Peter in Rome, which were recorded by Mark. Following Peter's death, these were assembled as Peter's Gospel (See Chapter 2 in *Evidence for the Bible*, Consider Christianity Series, Volume 1).

191 Martin, *Case*, p. 97-100

192 Martin does argue that even if you accept that Jesus rose from the dead, this does not prove that God exists, or that Jesus' claims are true. This goes back to the first chapter and our discussion of the impossibility of absolute proof. Still, while it may not absolutely prove that Jesus is God, the resurrection is very strong evidence that Jesus statements can be trusted.

The biblical accounts state that Jesus died on the cross and rose again on the third day. Do the critics have a better explanation for these events?

Throughout history, many theories have attempted to provide an alternative explanation for the resurrection, which would not require a belief in God or the supernatural. We can summarize these into five groups: Theft, Wrong Tomb, Twin, Hallucinations, and Swoon theories.

Theft of the Body

The earliest alternative explanation for the resurrection was someone stole the body of Jesus, allowing the disciples to claim that there had been a resurrection. Matthew states in his Gospel that the early critics of Christianity were spreading this theory.

The theories involving the theft of the body are divided into two main groups: those where the disciples steal the body and those in which the disciples are genuinely unaware.

Since the Theft theory originated just after the resurrection, it reveals one of the key facts that must be dealt with by any explanation: the tomb was empty. If the tomb were not empty, then the early critics would have had only to produce the body to disprove the Christian claims.

On the other hand, why would the opponents have needed to allege theft if he was buried in a mass grave and his body lost? It would seem that there was a particular tomb that at one time contained the body of Jesus but now does not. As critic Michael Grant admits:

> Even if the historian chooses to regard the youthful apparitions as extra-historical, he cannot justifiably deny the empty tomb... if we apply the same sort of criteria that we would apply to any other ancient literary sources, then the evidence is firm and plausible enough to necessitate the conclusion that the tomb was indeed found empty.[193]

193 Michael Grant, *Jesus: An Historian's Review of the Gospels* (New York:

Grant believes that someone other than the disciples took Jesus' body. But if this was the case, then who? Even more importantly, why would they take it? What possible purpose is there for anyone who was not a disciple for stealing the body of Jesus? Grant provides no answer to these questions.

Some have suggested that Pontius Pilate removed the body to prevent the disciples of Jesus from martyring themselves at the grave site. One early theory even indicated that a gardener removed the body because he did not want the disciples trampling upon his newly planted lettuce crop! These are hardly viable solutions. In addition, if someone other than the disciples took the body, why wasn't this revealed when the disciples claimed Jesus had risen?

There are even more significant problems with the theory that the disciples were responsible for the theft. One problem is that, by all accounts, the disciples were scattered and afraid after the death of Jesus, and they were in no position to carry out such a theft. Even if they had, how would they have gotten past the guards?

Because of the problem caused by the presence of guards at the tomb, some critics have claimed that they were a literary creation by Matthew to make the resurrection harder to disprove. While this may sound reasonable to those who accept the Theft theory, what facts support such a contention?

If the guards were simply a literary creation, why doesn't Matthew have at least some of them become Christians? They could have testified to the resurrection instead of saying someone stole the body.

Written while there were still people alive who remembered these events, the most likely explanation for the account in Matthew is that there were guards at the tomb. They were spreading stories about the theft of the body, and Matthew felt he needed to respond to these claims.

The main reason for rejecting Matthew's account concerning the guards is that it makes the resurrection too difficult to dismiss.

Charles Scribner's Sons, 1977) p. 176

Of course, if you selectively choose which biblical accounts are "correct" and which are "later additions," you can make this theory tenable. This is not formulating an opinion to fit the evidence but formulating the evidence to fit an opinion.

Another factor is the disciples' willingness to die for their beliefs. While all the disciples suffered torture or died violent deaths, none ever renounced their faith. Martin finds this argument "difficult to understand."[194] He points out that,

> People who have *not* claimed to be eyewitnesses to Jesus' appearances have also been transformed into people who were willing to die for their Christian beliefs. Let us not forget either that Muslims, Mormons, followers of James Jones, Kamikaze pilots, and many others have been willing to die for what they believed (Author's italics).[195]

Yet Martin seems to have missed the point entirely. The argument is not that people dying for what they believe somehow makes it true. Many people die for their beliefs in war, yet both sides cannot be correct. The real question is not whether people will die for what they believe is true, but will they die for what they know to be a lie?

Those who were eyewitnesses to Jesus' resurrection did not just believe what others had told them; they had seen it for themselves or at least thought they had. They would have known it was a hoax if they had stolen the body. Is it likely that the disciples and others who claimed to have witnessed the resurrection would have endured such torture? Would they willingly face death for what they knew to be a lie?

When taken together, the problems of who stole the body, why they stole it, and how they could have stolen it renders the Theft theory untenable as a valid alternative explanation for the resurrection.

---

194 Martin, *Case*, p. 91
195 Martin, *Case*, p. 91

The Wrong Tomb

Another attempt at solving the problem of the empty tomb is the theory that the women went to the wrong tomb on that first Easter morning. Supporters of this theory point out that Jesus was buried late on Friday afternoon, and the evening was approaching. It must have been getting dark when Joseph and Nicodemus placed Jesus' body in the tomb.

Because of this, supporters of this theory claim that the women would not have been able to see the tomb's location very clearly. When they tried to return on early Sunday morning, it was also dark, and as a result, they ended up at the wrong tomb.

Like the others, this theory also has several problems. Even if we assume for the moment that the women did go to the wrong tomb, how is it that no one ever discovered their mistake? Are we to believe no one ever bothered to check on their discovery? Did Peter and John also go to the wrong tomb?

If the women went to the wrong tomb, then the body of Jesus would still have been in the tomb owned by Joseph of Arimathea.[196] If so, why didn't the Sanhedrin go to Joseph's tomb and bring out the body when the disciples began proclaiming the resurrection throughout Jerusalem?

Why did the guards spread the story of the theft of the body? The Wrong Tomb theory raises more questions than answers and is not a viable explanation.

---

196 As for the possibility that Joseph of Arimathea made a mistake and placed Jesus in the wrong tomb, it is virtually impossible that Joseph would have been so confused as to not know the way to his own tomb, even on the darkest of nights, much less at dusk. If somehow he had made a mistake and went to the wrong tomb, once inside he would have noticed that the tomb he was in was not his own.

Twin

According to the Twin theory, Jesus had a twin brother. After His death, Jesus' twin brother appeared to the disciples and not Jesus Himself. Again, this theory has many problems.

One is that the theory has no basis of support. Nowhere is there any indication that Jesus had a twin brother. Was His mother in on the deception? Jesus' close relatives, who were critical of His ministry while He was alive, also proclaimed the resurrection. Presumably, they would have known about any twin brother. Were they in on this plot, or were they also deceived?

What about Thomas, who would not believe "unless I see the nail marks in his hands and put my finger where the nails were" (John 20:25). Jesus showed Thomas His hands and side, and Thomas believed. Would a twin have been able, or wanted, to duplicate these wounds?

Another problem with the Twin theory is that it says nothing about the empty tomb. If Jesus had a twin brother impersonating him after his death, how is it that no one checked the tomb? Why didn't Saul, who was doing everything he could to stop the church, produce the body of Jesus and disprove the resurrection? The Twin theory does not stand up to scrutiny.

Hallucinations

A fourth group of theories centers around believing that the disciples did not actually see Jesus. Instead, they only thought they saw him – they hallucinated. Historian Charles Guignebert summarized this theory as follows,

> The disciples returned to Galilee perplexed, troubled and afraid; discouraged, too, because none of their hopes had been realized and they had sustained a crushing blow... The promised future which had attracted and bound them to Jesus was bound up with his person: to admit that he had disappeared forever was to abandon all hope. Their faith was centered in, and, we might say, hypnotized by this idea: it is not possible

that he should be irrevocably dead. Such a tension of desire
and faith in the minds and hearts of uncultured men... have
only one logical outcome – the occurrence of visions.[197]

Ian Wilson presented a somewhat different twist to this theory
when he contented that Jesus used his skill as a magician trained
in Egypt. Using what amounted to a posthypnotic suggestion, he
caused his followers to believe that they had seen the risen Lord.

As with the Twin theory, the Hallucination theory says nothing
about the empty tomb or what happened to the body. It also faces
difficulties in that the resurrection was experienced by more than
just a single person.

Are we to believe that the two men on the road to Emmaus
simultaneously experience the same hallucination? What about the
disciples? Did they all simultaneously share the same hallucination?
They saw Jesus several times. What about the skeptical Thomas?
Was each occurrence the result of a mass hallucination?

As for the posthypnotic suggestion, it would be tough to con-
ceive how the actual mechanics of this could take place. Even if you
ignore the fact of the empty tomb, how do you, using posthypnotic
suggestion, account for over 500 people seeing Jesus at the same
time? As we have seen, Paul, in one of his earliest letters, referred
to this event as evidence for the resurrection (1 Corinthians 15:6).

Another issue for the Hallucination theories is the apostle Paul
himself. Often, critics argued that only Jesus' disciples claimed
to have seen Him. Yet, when Paul encountered Jesus, he did not
believe Him to be the Messiah.

He was not hoping for Jesus to return. On the contrary, he
was glad that Jesus was dead. Paul devoted his life to ending the
movement that Jesus had started.

Still, he saw the risen Jesus. What was it that caused his hallucination? As with the other theories, the Hallucination theory
does not fit the evidence.

---

197 Guignebert, *Jesus*, p. 527

Swoon Theory

The last group of theories we will examine comes from the premise that Jesus did not die on the cross but lived through the crucifixion. One version of this theory is that Jesus simply fainted while on the cross. The guards then mistook Him for dead, removed His body, and allowed Joseph and Nicodemus to bury him.

While in the tomb, Jesus regained consciousness and simply left; this explains the empty tomb. The "resurrection appearances" were then made by Jesus after He had regained His health. According to this view, the "resurrection" was simply a lucky break.

Another version of the Swoon theory sees the resurrection not as a lucky break but as a deliberate plan. The most well-known proponent of this theory is Hugh Schonfield, who detailed this position in his books *The Passover Plot* and *After the Cross*.

According to Schonfield, Jesus planned his arrest and trial so that He would be crucified late on Friday afternoon. Since the bodies would not be up over the Passover, He would be on the cross for only a few hours.

He would call for a drink at the appropriate time, and the guards would give him a sponge. Typically, it would contain vinegar, but this sponge had a drug to simulate death.

The plan was to place Jesus in the tomb until after the Sabbath. At that time, Joseph of Arimathea would return and take Him to the Essene community, where they could nurse him back to health. Jesus would then reappear, proclaiming His resurrection.

Things did not go as planned. One of the guards became suspicious and decided to see if Jesus was really dead. He took his spear and thrust it into Jesus' side, ending all hope for a recovery. Schonfield writes:

> We might then postulate that Jesus did recover conscious-
> ness not long after he had been conveyed to some suitable
> place for treatment, and that his first thought was for the sor-
> row of his followers who believed him to be dead. He would

certainly wish to get word to them that he was alive. Resurrection does not apply here, since Jesus had not in fact died. Later, of course, he could have had a relapse and expired.[198]

Another recent theory by Holger Kersten and Elmar Gruber agrees that Jesus planned his crucifixion so that he could survive it. They, however, suggest that Jesus had studied yoga techniques to control pain[199] and that the wound to the side was only "a minor scratch."[200] They also claim the guard who gave him the wine was in on the plot[201] and that the spices used to wrap his body were medicines to heal his wounds.

All of these theories, by necessity, have Jesus retiring from public life. Some claim that Jesus stayed in Israel and died during the Roman siege of Masada. Another theory is that Jesus and Mary Magdalene headed east to find the ten lost tribes of Israel.[202]

Mary made it as far as Pakistan, where she died, while Jesus continued and finally died in Kashmir.[203] Still, another theory is that Jesus settled down with His family after the crucifixion. According to this theory, he married Mary Magdalene and settled in Marseilles in the south of France.[204]

The swoon theories all suffer from two significant difficulties, either one of which is a sufficient reason for rejecting them. First, how could Jesus have survived the crucifixion? Second, how could He have left the tomb?

---

198 Hugh Schonfield, *After the Cross* (New York: A S Barnes & Co, 1981) p. 64

199 Holger Kersten and Elmar Gruber, *The Jesus Conspiracy: The Turin Shroud & the Truth About the Resurrection* (Rockport, MA, Element, 1994) p. 246

200 Kersten, *Jesus*, pg 251

201 Kersten, *Jesus*, pg 248, 253

202 A. Faber-Kaiser, *Jesus Died in Kashmir* (London: Gordon & Cremonesi, 1977) p. 76

203 Faber-Kaiser, *Jesus*, pp. 82 & 96

204 M. Baigent, R. Leigh and H. Lincoln, *Holy Blood, Holy Grail* (New York: Delacorte Press, 1982) pp. 325-332

Perhaps the most severe problem for the Swoon theory is the belief that Jesus could have survived the cross. As evidence that He could, supporters point to a passage in the writings of the Jewish historian, Josephus.

Josephus tells us that after seeing three of his friends crucified, he pleaded for their release. The authorities granted his requests. He immediately had the three men removed from the cross and given medical attention.

While two of these men died, the third did survive. Supporters point to this third man as proof that a person can survive crucifixion and that the Swoon theory is at least possible.

While this may seem reasonable at first glance, a closer examination reveals some serious flaws. One problem is that the third man did not have to fake his death on the cross to avoid having his legs broken.

When someone is crucified, the pressure on the nails in the hands causes spasms in the chest, making breathing impossible. The only way to breathe is to place all their weight on the nail through their feet, relieving pressure on the arms and chest muscles and making breathing possible.

When the legs are broken, this is no longer possible, and the person dies of suffocation within a few minutes.[205] If Jesus had fainted or drugged into unconsciousness, the result would have been the same as breaking his legs. Jesus would have no longer been able to stand up and thus would not have been able to breathe, and he would have died very quickly.

Another indication that Jesus died is in the book of John. John states that when the guard thrust his spear into the side of Jesus, there was "a sudden flow of blood and water" (John 19:34). This sudden flow of blood, followed by water, led doctors investigating the effects of crucifixion, to conclude that Jesus died of a ruptured heart.[206]

---

205 Josh McDowell, *The Resurrection Factor* (San Bernardino, CA: Here's Life, 1981) pp. 46-8
206 McDowell, *Resurrection*, pp. 48-49

An article in the *Journal of the American Medical Association* summed up the situation as follows,

Clearly, the weight of historical and medical evidence indicates that Jesus was dead before the wound to His side was inflicted and supports the traditional view that the spear, thrust between His right ribs, probably perforated not only the right lung but also the pericardium and heart and thereby ensured his death. Accordingly, interpretations based on the assumption that Jesus did not die on the cross appear to be at odds with modern medical knowledge.[207]

There can be little doubt that Jesus died on the cross. Many of these theories simply will not work.

For example, Kersten and Gruber decided to test some of their theories by duplicating some of the conditions they believe Jesus went through in the tomb. Yet, they were only partially successful.

Kersten writes, "For one thing, I could not remain lying in a sweat without moving for hours - a short period of this and I was near circulatory collapse."[208] But one must ask, if Kersten, who was in good health, could not survive this process, how are we to believe that Jesus could survive after being beaten and crucified?

The second problem faced by the Swoon theory is that even if by some miracle, and it would have been a miracle, Jesus did get off the cross alive, how did he survive in the tomb? How did he get out?

If the cross had not killed him, surely he would have died had he been left unattended in the tomb after the crucifixion. Only one of the three men saved by Josephus survived, and they all received medical treatment immediately. So even if Jesus had survived the cross, He would have died in the tomb.

If he had survived the cross and was still alive on Sunday morning, how could he have gotten out of the tomb? In his weakened condition, there would have been no natural way for Jesus

207 William D. Edwards, M.D., et al., On the Physical Death of Jesus Christ *Journal of the American Medical Association*, 255:11, March 21, 1986, p. 1463 cited in, Norman Geisler and Ron Brooks, *When Skeptics Ask: A Handbook on Christian Evidences* (Wheaton, Ill: Victor Books, 1990) p. 123
208 Kersten, *Jesus*, pg 299

to have moved the stone covering the entrance, much less get past the guards.

Suppose he had help from one or more of his disciples. This claim simply leads back to the theories centered around the theft of the body and all the problems they encounter. As we have already seen, the theft theories do not hold up.

If, by some miracle, Jesus had survived the cross and escaped the tomb, He would have been on the verge of death. Could Jesus have inspired His followers as the risen Lord in such a condition? If this had been the case, the Gospels would have contained accounts of the miracle of Jesus escaping death, not conquering it. So, the Swoon theory also fails to stand up under examination.

Conclusion

We have examined each of the theories put forth by the critics of Christianity, and none of them can explain the events of that first Easter morning. The supporters of these different theories see certain historical aspects in the Gospel accounts. The problem is that they cannot agree on which parts are historical and which are not.

Many critics accept the empty tomb as being a historical event. While they may dispute the exact details of the events described in the Gospels, they acknowledge that Jesus' tomb was empty. As we saw earlier, the historian Michael Grant wrote,

> if we apply the same sort of criteria that we would apply to any other ancient literary sources, then the evidence is firm and plausible enough to necessitate the conclusion that the tomb was indeed found empty.[209]

Other critics believe that the empty tomb was nothing more than a creation by the Gospel writers. Guignebert states,

> the discovery of the empty tomb, useless as far as the disciples' faith is concerned, falls into the category of an apologetic

---

209 Grant, *Jesus*, p. 176

or polemical invention and is eliminated from the realm of history.[210]

The only thing critics can seem to agree on is that the accounts presented in the Gospels are wrong. This rejection is based not so much on the evidence that the resurrection did not happen but the belief that it could not happen. Guignebert writes,

> When once the purely miraculous hypothesis has been discarded, support for all kinds of hypotheses may be found in the sources, because they favor none of them... This is a problem which every student solves according to his understanding of it, with varying degrees of probability; but the point must be emphasized that these probabilities themselves depend on a process of imagination; the sources neither give nor suggest them.[211]

After reviewing a number of these alternative explanations and showing them to be inadequate, Wilson writes,

> If the hypothesis that Jesus did rise from the grave is set aside as being impossible to prove, the only remaining theory meriting further consideration is that the disciples somehow hallucinated.[212]

Unfortunately for Wilson, the Hallucination theory does not provide a satisfactory explanation.

In the *Sign of Four*, Sherlock Holmes remarked to Watson, "when you have eliminated the impossible, whatever remains, however improbable, must be the truth."[213] What Holmes pointed out is known in logic as a disjunctive syllogism or, more commonly, the process of elimination.

We have examined the many alternative theories for the resurrection, but none satisfactorily explain what happened that first

210 Guignebert, *Jesus*, p. 500
211 Guignebert, Jesus, p. 513-14
212 Wilson, Jesus, p. 141
213 Sir Author Conan Doyle, *The Sign of Four* in *The Complete Sherlock Holmes* (New York: Doubleday, 1988) p. 111

Easter morning. Some critics view the empty tomb as the critical historical event needing an explanation. They regard the appearances as later literary creations.

Other critics believe the appearances are historical and regard the empty tomb as a literary creation. A few see both events as literary creations. The evidence supports none of these theories.

Christians believe both the empty tomb and the appearances are historical events. Since Christians are not philosophically biased against the supernatural, they see no reason to try to explain away these events.

They accept them for what they report: Jesus Christ was crucified, died, was buried, and then rose from the dead.

Despite the critics' claims, the New Testament presents a clear, consistent testimony of these events. As Christian historian Paul Maier has written,

> Many facts from antiquity rest on just one ancient source, while two or three sources in agreement generally render the fact unimpeachable. In the case of the first Easter, there are at least *seven* ancient sources – the four Gospels, Acts, and the letters of Paul and Peter – but this has not led to universal acceptance of the resurrection as a datum of history. Why not? Because the more unlikely the story, the stronger the evidence demanded for it. So if something supernatural were claimed, the evidence required to support it would have to be of an unimpeachable, absolute, and indeed, direct eyewitness nature. Quite obviously, however, such categorical evidence disappeared with the death of the last eyewitnesses nineteen centuries ago.[214]

If it were not for the supernatural nature of the accounts, then the resurrection of Jesus would be one of history's most established and unimpeachable facts.

---

214 Paul L Maier, *First Easter* in *The Historical Jesus: A Scholarly View of the Man and His World* Ed, Gaalyah Cornfeld (New York: Macmillan, 1982) p. 183

The resurrection is the only explanation that fits all the evidence. In addition, a historical resurrection would explain the transformation of Jesus' followers from a crushed and defeated group without a leader into a dynamic and growing church whose members were willing to suffer death rather than renounce their belief in a risen Lord.

What happened that first Easter morning? The evidence supports only one conclusion. Jesus, a religious leader executed for claiming to be God incarnate, conquered death and rose again, leaving behind an empty tomb. Many people saw him, and some were not followers of His but became followers as a result. After forty days, Jesus ascended into Heaven, promising to return during the last days. The evidence supports Christians when they proclaim: Christ is risen!

Part III

Christianity

And The

Modern World

7

Is Christianity Relevant?

Reason cannot establish values, and its belief that it can is the stupidest and most pernicious illusion.

(Allan Bloom)[215]

IT TOOK A hard man to be a slave trader, but John Newton did not have an easy life. He was born in 1725, and his mother died when he was only seven. When he was eleven, he went to sea aboard a Royal Navy ship.

However, John and the Navy did not get along very well, so he decided on a career change – unfortunately, without the consent of the Royal Navy. When His Majesty's government finally caught up with John in West Africa, they flogged him and sent him to sea again aboard a slave ship.

Life at sea was not easy under the best of circumstances. Life on a slave ship was a living hell. Everywhere on the ship, there were slaves chained together and suffering. Many slaves would die on the voyage, so slavers packed their ships as tightly as possible to ensure enough would survive to make the trip profitable.

John soon hardened himself to the suffering around him. When he finished his forced service, he remained in the slave trade. While it was a cruel and inhumane business, there was, after all, money to be made. He worked his way up through the ranks until, in 1750, he got command of his own ship.

---

215 Allan Bloom, *The Closing of the American Mind* (New York: Simon and Schuster, 1987) p. 194

John was a hard man, but he was not beyond the reach of God. On one particularly rough trip across the Atlantic, John began to read *Imitation of Christ*, a book written by a fifteenth-century Dutch monk.

Before the voyage was over, he had accepted Jesus as his Lord and Savior. It is not uncommon to see people react to adversity by turning to God, but for John, this was more than just a "foxhole conversion." While foxhole conversions fade quickly once the adversity is over, John's conversion affected his entire life, changing it forever.

Like many before him, at first, John tried to make Christianity fit into his old way of life by holding worship services for the crew of his slave ship. Before long, however, he could not escape the brutal nature of his business.

John gave up the slave trade and returned to England. Yet, he did not return home to worship quietly. Instead, because of his newfound faith, John became a strong and vocal opponent of slavery.

In 1785, he helped persuade a recent convert, William Wilberforce, to stay in public office so he could fight the evils of slavery and eventually end it.

However, John Newton is best remembered for his music. It was perhaps because he was once a hardened slave trader that he could write the following lines from one of the most famous of all Christian hymns,

> *Amazing Grace, how sweet the sound,*
> *that saved a wretch like me*
> *For once I was lost*
> *But now I am found*
> *Was blind, but now can see.*

Christianity changed John Newton's life and played an essential role in shaping his society, including abolishing slavery. While Christianity may have had a dramatic effect on people in the past, some now claim that regardless of whether or not Christianity is true, it is no longer relevant.

Some argue that the Bible was written to people who lived thousands of years ago. They centered their lives around the farm. Today's society focuses on the city, emphasizing science and technology.

Since the Bible, we have learned so much that those alive today have little in common with those who lived 2000 years ago. Therefore, even if the Bible is historically reliable, it has little value to people living in an age of computers and space exploration.

A fundamental premise of this argument is that the Bible's message is inseparably linked to the culture of the time. Obviously, this is true to some extent.

The Bible is not a book of systematic theology. It teaches by example and illustration, reflecting the specific cultural settings of the times.

Yet the questions dealt with in the Bible transcend culture and address universal issues. According to the Bible, the main problem confronting the apostle Paul was the same problem facing John Newton and the same problem facing people today: sin.[216]

A Small Matter of Sin

The Bible's core message is that people are sinful and need salvation. Jesus Christ came, died, and rose again to provide that salvation. This is the Gospel.

It has nothing to do with the cultural setting of the time but is universal. The fact that Christianity has lasted for nearly 2000 years demonstrates this. It has spread worldwide and into multiple and vastly different cultures.

Looking at our society, there is no indication that the central problem addressed in the Bible, sin, is any less of a problem today than it was 2000 years ago. The issues of crime, drugs, violence, and corruption have not diminished over the years. Even a casual perusal of the news will show that sin is as big a problem now as ever.

---

216 For a definition of sin see the section on salvation in chapter three.

Some object to the use of the term "sin" as being too religious. They prefer to use words like "ethics" and "morality." While there is very little concern over sin, there is a lot of concern over ethics.

Ethics classes are now the norm in college and business. Ethics boards have been established at many hospitals to help doctors make difficult decisions.

Yet, with all the discussion about ethics, there is virtually no mention of God or religion. Moral authority is transferred from God to the professor of ethics at the local university or appropriate ethics board. There seems to be a belief that moral or ethical decisions have no religious significance. These decisions are separate from religion.

Until recently, most Western cultures had a common perception that morality was a set of principles of right and wrong that originated from God. These principles were an external standard by which we could judge people's actions. Even those who did not believe in God still thought religion was essential to maintain morality.

There were differences in the exact details of these principles and various views concerning the nature of God. But overall, there was agreement – at least on the general tenets of right and wrong. Now, with religion removed from the equation and with the foundation gone, morality is suffering.

Personal Morality?

In place of fixed external standards given by God, we now have relative standards of personal morality[217] that change from person to person and situational ethics that vary from one situation to the next. In one respect, situational ethics is nothing new. Most systems of morality based on God consider the situation in which events occur.

---

217 The phrase *personal morality* is being used in the modern sense of referring to a person's moral standards, as opposed to the earlier sense of one's level of commitment to a set of objective moral principles.

It is wrong to break the law, and it is also wrong to let a child die if you can save them. Suppose you saw a child drowning in a pool, but the pool was in a yard marked 'No Trespassing.' The greater good would be to save the child's life, even if it meant breaking the law and trespassing onto private property. Not trespassing to save the child would be considered morally wrong.

What is new about situational ethics is not the application of moral principles to a given situation but rather that the problem *determines* the moral principles. With situational ethics, moral principles such as those from God are no longer objective. Instead, they are relative, determined by the person to fit a particular situation. Morality becomes genuinely personal, but can morality be left to the individual?

Hitler felt his situation justified the killing of 11 million people in concentration camps.[218] Stalin felt his need to maintain control in the Soviet Union gave him the right to kill between 25 and 60 million people.[219] China's rulers thought they needed to use force against the pro-democracy movement in Tiananmen Square. Whites in South Africa felt their situation justified imposing the system of apartheid.

Most people feel that their situation justifies their actions. So why are these actions wrong, but ours right when we say ours are justified? This question is one of the reasons that most philosophers do not accept situational ethics. It does not hold up under scrutiny.

If morality is determined by the individual, based on their situation, then when would anything ever be wrong? If morality is relative, it becomes basically impossible to say anything is wrong.

---

218 The estimates for the number of people who died in the concentration camps vary considerably. That six million Jews were killed is well established, but many others also died in the camps. Estimates range to has high as 25 million. see *Encyclopedia Britannica*, 15th ed. (1978), s.v. *concentration camp*
219 Mikhail Heller & Aleksandr M. Nekrich, *Utopia in Power: The History of the Soviet Union from 1917 to Present* (New York: Summit Books, 1986) p. 511

Morality would cease to be clear principles of right and wrong but instead would be matters of personal preference.

We would have no basis from which to condemn the actions of others, including a Hitler or a Stalin. The strongest statement we could logically make would be to say that it would not have been our personal choice to kill millions of people, but then, who are we to judge the actions of others?

Morality or Convenience

Suppose a country's leader faces a choice to kill millions of people; how should they come to a decision? With situational ethics, the decision cannot be grounded on right and wrong, for that will be the result of the decision, not the foundation. The leader must decide on some other basis. Typically, the decision will come from what is most convenient for the person.

Fortunately, while the belief that morality is relative is prevalent,[220] it has not yet fully integrated into our society. Like a large glacier moving down a hill, society does not change direction quickly. Even though many ignore the foundation for morality, much of the old morality remains, and external standards still play an essential role in decision-making. Still, the decline over the last several decades is evident.

With the change, the new external standard is increasingly the law. Where once politicians caught in a scandal used to claim they did nothing wrong, now they claim they did nothing illegal. Lawyers teach many ethics classes in schools and businesses, and in some cases, being a lawyer is a job requirement to teach the course. What matters is not whether something is right or wrong but is legal.

For instance, while many people may consider morality relative, most would have little trouble condemning an adult who had sexual relations with a child. But without an external standard upon

---

220 In a recent survey 67% agreed with the statement "There is no such thing as absolute truth; different people can define truth in conflicting ways." George Barna, *What Americans Believe* (Ventura, CA: Regal Books, 1991) p. 83

which to base moral decisions, there is little justification for this condemnation beyond it being illegal.

Some might claim this is morally wrong because the child is not old enough to consent. But why should consent be necessary if there is no external basis for morality? If we are consistent in rejecting external standards, we cannot consider an adult having sexual relations with a child to be morally wrong. It would simply be something we choose not to do.

But even here, the moral decay is noticeable since the comments above appeared in the first edition of this book. When I wrote the first edition in the early nineties, I worried the example might be too extreme to be believable.

Since then, there has been a small but growing movement in this area. The push to lower the age of consent has moved beyond groups such as the NAMBLA – the North American Man Boy Love Association – gaining some, if limited, following. In Europe, the trend has been for lowering the age of consent, in some cases to as low as twelve.

If taken to its logical conclusion, with personal morality, no action, whether lying to a friend or murdering millions of people, would be inherently immoral or wrong. They would be matters of personal choice where the only limiting factor was the law.

The logical question would be: If nothing is inherently wrong but only a matter of personal choice, why should we have any laws? If stealing is not wrong, why should we have laws against theft? While initially written as a purely rhetorical question, in recent years, a few have raised this argument in the face of rising theft. Surprisingly, or perhaps not, we are seeing this thinking play out, with cities reducing or even dropping criminal penalties and crime skyrocketing.

In logic, this type of argument is called *reductio ad absurdum*. You demonstrate a problem in a position by showing that when carried out logically, the position becomes absurd. The belief that morality has no external basis becomes absurd when carried to its logical conclusions.

Any system of morality that cannot even assert that the concentration camps of Hitler and Stalin were inherently immoral has to be seriously flawed. There must be some sort of external basis for morality, something other than our subjective personal opinions, upon which to base our decisions concerning right and wrong, good and evil.

A Firm Foundation?

How can we determine right from wrong? What is good from what is evil? Many have attempted to find a foundation for morality that does not involve religion or faith. All have ultimately failed. This failure is because there are only three areas from which a foundation for morality[221] can come: nature, public consensus, or religion.

During the latter part of the nineteenth century and the first half of the twentieth, there was great interest in applying the lessons of nature, like survival of the fittest, to human society and morality.

These attempts proved disastrous when they resulted in the emergence of the eugenics movement in science, the rise of Nazi Germany, and the idea of a master race. Since World War II, few have considered nature a foundation for morality.

If, on the other hand, you look to public consensus as a way of judging what is right and wrong, the obvious question becomes: A consensus of whom? Is it the public as a whole? Is it some elite group whose job is to make moral judgments for the rest of us?

If so, on what basis are they to make their decisions? The elite group seems to be the trend, with ethical committees or judges being the elites who make these decisions. However, using consensus as a basis for morality has many problems.

Let's look at a somewhat extreme example to remove ambiguity and see the problems. Most people would agree that torturing babies for fun is morally wrong. The real question would be, is torturing babies for fun wrong only because most people agree that it is, or is

---

221 We are concerned here only with the foundation of morality and not the development of moral systems which come under the realm of philosophy.

it inherently wrong? If someone could get a consensus approving of torturing babies for fun, would that suddenly make it right?

Suppose you believe that something about torturing babies for fun is inherently wrong, regardless of what the latest public opinion poll might say. In that case, you are not using consensus as a basis for moral decisions.

Morality based on consensus suffers from the same problems as morality based on the individual. Ultimately, they both reduce to statements of preferences rather than guiding principles to judge human behavior.

Since nature and consensus cannot provide a solid basis for moral decisions, the principles of right and wrong must come from religion. All moral questions are, in the final analysis, religious questions.

A Question of Rights?

Some might claim that religion is not necessary to show that torturing babies for fun is wrong because it violates the human rights of those tortured. While I agree torturing babies for fun violates the human rights of the victims, what are human rights, and where do they come from?

Currently, the foundation of human rights is a significant question for the world community. Are human rights simply the rights granted to us by a government, like those in the U.S. Bill of Rights?

If so, what if a government did not grant those rights? Would that mean that the rights would not exist? If the concept of rights is to mean anything at all, then they cannot be what is granted by the government. If they were, they would be legal grants, not human rights, subject to the whim of those in power.

Governments may or may not recognize human rights but do not grant them. We must have human rights because we are human for them to be meaningful. But from where do rights come? Why do we have rights to life and free speech?

The question of the origin of human rights is the same as the origin of morality. Human rights have their foundation in religion, either traditional or secular.

The religious roots are evident in the Declaration of Independence's claim that "all men are created equal, endowed by their Creator with certain inalienable rights." The principal author of the United Nations' *Universal Declaration of Human Rights*, René Cassin, acknowledged that the Ten Commandments were the ideological basis for that document.[222]

The religious backing of morality or human rights may be hidden by tradition or labeled as common sense. Still, when examined, the origins of the traditions will be religious. For Western civilization, the moral traditions go back to Moses and Jesus and are called the Judeo-Christian heritage.

Whether moral principles are given by God or derived from spiritual principles, religion provides the foundation and stability to morality needed to maintain a civilization. As we move further away from the religious foundations of morality, society's problems get progressively worse.

This reasoning does not mean that only people who believe in God are moral. A person can be an atheist and still be a very moral person who does a tremendous amount of good.

The real question is, from where do morals come? An atheist can choose whatever moral values they want within the constraints of the broader society. If raised in a culture where religiously based morals still exert a strong influence, they could choose those moral values. But they don't have to. They will likely accept only some of these moral principles while rejecting others.

In a society where moral decisions are not grounded in religion, morals will slowly decay as most of the population's accepted ethical principles become progressively smaller.

For the atheist or the theist who believes God plays no role in morality, it is all a matter of choice. They can choose values con-

---

222 John Warwick Montgomery, *Human Rights and Human Dignity* (Dallas, TX: Probe Books, 1986) p. 30

sidered good, but they can also just as easily choose values deemed evil. Without religion, it is all a matter of personal choice.

In the fifties, one of the major problems in public schools was chewing gum. Since then, there has been a solid and largely successful movement to secularize society. The belief in the separation of church and state has extended to morality.

Should we really be surprised that today the problems in school include murder, drugs, gangs, rape, and assault? In 1989, Los Angeles built a ten-foot-high wall around one school to keep stray bullets from killing children as they played at recess,[223] and things have only gotten worse since then.

Since I wrote this example in the first edition, there, unfortunately, have been several examples of kids taking guns to schools and killing their fellow students and teachers. I could give numerous other examples of decay; sadly, the children often suffer the most.

Many studies on the state of children show growing problems. Teenage depression and suicide are increasing issues, and gang violence and drug deaths among teens are also significant problems. As such, it is not hard to seriously wonder if society can survive without some firm moral basis.

Christianity is not only true, but it is also relevant and needed. This statement is not as revolutionary as it may appear at first glance. Most would agree that religions encourage people to be good and that religious people are less likely to do evil.

Dennis Prager, in a debate with Jonathan Glover at Oxford University in March 1993, drove this point home with the following question:

> Imagine you are walking in a bad Los Angeles neighborhood at midnight. You are alone, and you notice ten men walking towards you in a dark alley. Would you or would you not be relieved to know that they had just attended a Bible class? ... while it is still possible they will mug or rape you, deep in your gut you know that the likelihood is that they won't.[224]

223 *Los Angles Times*, April 15 or 16 1989 p. 1
224 Dennis Prager and Jonathan Glover, *Can We Be Good Without God? A*

We can see a similar attitude reflected in the often-heard statement that the world would be much better if only people would follow the Ten Commandments or the moral teachings of Jesus. A lot of people like the moral teachings of Jesus; they just don't like all the "religious stuff" accompanying it. The problem is you cannot logically separate the two.

The problem of morality is, in reality, a spiritual problem, the root of which is sin. Any attempt to accept the moral teachings of Jesus while rejecting His religious teachings, is doomed to failure.

This is because Jesus did not compartmentalize his teachings to allow you to pick and choose among them. To reject the "religious stuff" is to reject the foundation for morality.

It is like telling a builder you like all the plans for a house, but they can skip the foundation. If you reject the foundation, ultimately, this leads to a rejection of the morality itself.

I'm sure that some will take what I have said concerning the importance of religion in maintaining society as a call for establishing Christianity as an official state religion. Nothing could be further from the truth.

Even if tomorrow, we changed the U.S. Constitution and Christianity became the official state religion, it would have little effect on society. In fact, it could be counterproductive.

Christianity is not concerned with society's problems as much as with the individual. While some call the United States a Christian country, it is because most citizens are Christian, and Christianity has strongly shaped its history and values.

In a literal sense, there is no such thing as a Christian country. One cannot impose Christianity on a group of people. No one is a Christian because they were born in a Christian nation, raised in a Christian home, or belong to a Christian group.

Becoming a Christian is not a social event. Christianity is a personal relationship between an individual and God. Any attempt to mandate Christianity will not work.

For Christianity to have a positive effect on society, as it has had in the past, it will be because it has positively impacted individuals. It is these individuals who then go on to affect society.

But no one can mandate that someone else become a Christian. No one can become a Christian through the choices or actions of another.

Individual Christianity

The choice rests with the individual, and it is a simple one. The problem that separates people from God is sin. "For all have sinned and fall short of the glory of God" (Romans 3:23).

The message of Jesus is unambiguous. No one is good enough to save themselves. Jesus, God the Son, Creator of the universe, and second person of the Trinity, became a man (Philippians 2:5-8), died for our sins, and rose again on the third day in victory over death.

Jesus paid the penalty for our sins so we would not have to. Our part of the bargain is that we accept and trust Jesus as our Savior. The choice is clear: we can either accept Jesus as our personal Savior and spend eternity with Him or reject Him and suffer eternal separation from God. The eternal separation from God is called Hell or the Lake of Fire.[225]

At this point, someone will probably complain that I am trying to use Hell to scare people into accepting Jesus. The argument is not with me, but with Jesus. In His teachings, Jesus talked more about avoiding Hell than He did about going to Heaven. The real question is what one means by trying to scare.

Suppose you live in a lovely house in a beautiful valley. I have just discovered that the dam has broken upstream, and a massive wall of water is rushing down the valley directly toward your home.

---

225 Technically, Hell is the place the unsaved currently go to upon death. After the final judgment, the unsaved will be cast along with Hell into the Lake of Fire. (Revelation 20:14)

If I came and told you of the disaster about to take place, would I be guilty of trying to scare you? Most people would say no. Rather than an attempt to scare, it is to warn.

Jesus, in His descriptions of hell, is not trying to scare us into a decision; instead, He is trying to warn us of the consequences of our decision.

Another common complaint is that it is somehow unfair that we need to choose at all. This complaint takes many forms. Usually, it comes along the lines that surely God would not send someone to hell simply because they did not believe everything Christians teach.

This argument misses the point entirely. God does not send anyone to hell simply because they do not accept what Christians say. Those who go to hell will go for one reason only: they separated themselves from God and refused His offer of salvation. After all, God sent His only Son to die on the cross to provide us with the means of salvation.

It would be like a person who got themselves trapped in a pit. You lower a rope down to them, which they reject. Then they claim that your offer is unfair and that they should not have to accept the rope to be free.

The problem is not belief or non-belief but rebellion against God. Belief is not the problem; believing in Jesus Christ as Savior is the solution.

Therefore, Jesus will not send anyone to hell simply because they did not believe all the correct theological doctrines. Instead, it will be because they wished to rebel against Him rather than accept His offer of salvation.

Another complaint is that it is unfair for God to force such a choice. After all, why doesn't God make a grand appearance, perform some miracles, and settle the issue of His existence once and for all?

Surely, it is within the power of an all-powerful God to prove beyond a shadow of a doubt that He does exist. While this is true to a certain degree, it neglects one of the fundamental principles taught in the Bible.

While it is true that God does have the power to meet any logical test that we could ask to prove His existence, it is also true that He does not. The skeptic concludes that God does not because He does not exist.

While that is one possible reason, what the skeptic neglects to consider is that God has given people free will and a chance to trust in Him. Just as we have free will to accept Him, we also have free will to reject Him. You cannot logically have one without the other. God does not force us to accept Him.

The question is not one of evidence, for as we have seen in this book and the previous book in this series, there is plenty of evidence to support the Christian position. The question is one of absolute proof.

The skeptic demands absolute proof, but this would not be compatible with a free choice. Do you have the free choice to choose whether or not $1 + 1 = 2$? Possibly, you might in some vague mathematical sense, but in any real and practical sense, no. Do you have a choice whether or not to accept the theory of gravity? No.

A demand for absolute proof is, in essence, a way of avoiding the need to make a decision. You no longer need to decide if someone provides you with absolute proof for a position. The choice is made for you. God does not want to choose for you; he wants you to accept and trust Him on your own.

To continue to demand absolute proof of the existence of God is simply a way of justifying rebellion. It says that you will not accept God until He meets your standards of empirical evidence. This attitude completely ignores that sin is the root of the problem.

It is not God who has rebelled against us. He does not need to meet our conditions for reconciliation. God is not the sinner who must seek our approval and meet our standards.

There is a further problem. As I show in my book *Seeking Truth*, the concept of absolute proof is an illusion. You can prove nothing absolutely, even that you exist. So, to demand absolute proof is to require the impossible.

Some might claim they are not in rebellion and have not rejected God. While an agnostic might argue that they have not made a decision, there is no such thing as a non-decision, for there is no middle ground.

Let us return to our story of the valley and the impending flood. Once warned of the flood, you can either believe the warning and act or reject it and do nothing; there is no middle ground.

There is no middle ground because only positive action, in this case, leaving the area, will save you. No decision is the same as a rejection. Both will leave you in the path of the flood.

The same is true for trusting in Jesus Christ as Savior. Because we are already rebelling against God, no decision is the same as rejecting Jesus. Both will leave you in a state of rebellion.

One of the most common objections concerns those who have never heard about Jesus. How can God require them to accept Jesus as Savior if they have never heard about Him?

This is not as great a problem as it might initially seem, for Paul tells us that God reveals Himself through nature.

> For since the creation of the world God's invisible qualities
> – his eternal power and divine nature – have been clearly seen,
> being understood from what has been made, so that men are
> without excuse. (Romans 1:20)

Someone who has never heard of Jesus Christ could still look at the world around them and realize a God must have created it. The Holy Spirit convicts them of their sin, just as He convicts us of ours (John 16:7). God is a just God, and he does not hold us responsible for things we could not possibly have known.

The situation of those who have never heard of Jesus is, I believe, very similar to those living before Jesus. Those alive before

Jesus did not know His name or that He would die on the cross for their sins. But those who lived before Jesus and trusted in God for their salvation were saved. Their salvation still comes through the blood of Christ, for that is the only means of salvation that God has provided.

There is also the question of people in other religions. If someone sincerely follows the teachings of a faith other than Christianity, are they saved? This question has two parts. The first concerns those in other religions who have never heard the Gospel. I believe this situation is the same as the one mentioned above. God's wisdom, mercy, and justice will decide each case.

As for those who have heard the Gospel, this is more complex. There is a difference between hearing the Gospel, understanding its meaning, and confronting its choice. We can see this more clearly by rephrasing the question: Can we simultaneously rely on Jesus as Savior and reject Jesus as Savior?

We must remember that Christianity is unique among the world's religions. Virtually all other religions depend on working hard so that you can be good enough to obtain whatever the goal of the religion.

Christianity, on the other hand, is not based on what you do. From God's point of view, "There is no one who does good, not even one" (Romans 3:12). Christianity depends on what Christ did for us. Jesus said, "My sheep listen to my voice; I know them and they follow me. I give them eternal life and they shall never perish" (John 10:27).

Suppose someone in another religion has genuinely turned from their rebellion against God. In that case, they will accept the Gospel when they hear it.[226]

---

226 Missionaries have reported this phenomenon. The first time that they go into a new area sometimes they will encounter people who readily accept the Gospel. On the other hand, there is a whole range of complicating issues dealing with how effectively the gospel was presented.

Because of factors such as this, when someone asks whether a particular person will go to heaven, I say that I do not know and cannot. I can learn the principles taught in the Bible about sin and salvation. Still, no one can honestly know what is in a person's heart or relationship with God. Nor can we understand the wisdom, mercy, and justice of God's judgments.

Conclusion

In the Introduction, we stated that this series attempts to show that Christianity is a rational, reasonable, and relevant religion. So far, we have seen that the evidence supports the Christian's claim that the Bible is the inspired Word of God, that Jesus is the Son of God, and that He did conquer death.

The evidence for Christianity is both strong and extensive. Critics have tried to disprove it on many fronts for nearly 2000 years, and none have succeeded.

In fact, few of these criticisms hold merit unless you start with the assumption that the supernatural does not exist. Christianity rests on a solid foundation of supportive evidence that does show it to be true. At the same time, the critics' arguments are founded more on opinions than facts.

For the non-Christian, there is a decision that you cannot ignore, for no decision is the same as a negative one. The evidence demonstrates that nearly 2000 years ago, God the Son entered the world as a man named Jesus. After a brief ministry, He died on the cross for our sins and was buried. He rose from the dead three days later.

Jesus offers you eternal life, purchased with His blood if you will, but turn from your rebellion, and in your own words, tell Him that you are trusting in him as your Savior. You can accept Jesus as your Savior, or you can reject Him. The choice is yours.

Index

www.ingramcontent.com/pod-product-compliance
Lightning Source LLC
Chambersburg PA
CBHW021226090426
42740CB00006B/393